WELCOME

With the new season about to begin, it's an exciting time to be a Formula 1 fan. This year marks the 75th anniversary of the sport, and its popularity is greater than ever. There has been a surge in viewership in recent years, with all the twists and turns of championship drama both on – and off – the track drawing in millions of fans all over the world.

In this special edition, we bring you everything you need to know about motor racing's high-speed thrills and awe-inspiring skills. If you're new to F1, why not start with our brief history of the sport, then check out the bluffer's guide to get to grips with the basics. Also inside, you can take a tour of the championship circuits, learn more about the teams and explore the drivers' hall of fame. If you want to discover more about what goes on behind the scenes, delve into the world of team strategies and the amazing technology behind the cars. Finally, you can look ahead to the future as we consider what to expect for the upcoming season, as well as what changes and challenges the sport can expect in years to come.

Whether you're an F1 newcomer or a lifelong fan, we hope you'll enjoy the ride!

CONTENTS

INTRODUCTION

- **8** — **75 YEARS OF FORMULA 1**
  A brief history of the sport
- **14** — **THE EVOLUTION OF AN F1 CAR**
  Compare the vehicles of 1950 and today
- **22** — **INNOVATIONS**
  How F1 tech has influenced road cars
- **26** — **BLUFFER'S GUIDE**
  New to F1? Here's what you need to know

8

90

TEAMS & DRIVERS

- **36** — **MEET THE TEAMS**
  An introduction to the ten constructors
- **52** — **F1 HALL OF FAME**
  Get to know the sport's most successful drivers
- **56** — **DRIVER TRAINING**
  What preparations drivers make for the season
- **66** — **TEAM TACTICS**
  Discover the strategies behind race success
- **70** — **PIT STOPS**
  How engineers perform ultra-fast stops
- **78** — **RIVALRIES**
  From friendly competition to driver drama
- **90** — **2024 SEASON REVIEW**
  Look back on how the last season unfolded

78 66

CONTENTS

16

CIRCUITS IN FOCUS

16	AUSTRALIA
18	CHINA
20	JAPAN
28	BAHRAIN
30	SAUDI ARABIA
32	MIAMI
46	IMOLA
48	MONACO
50	SPAIN
60	CANADA
62	AUSTRIA
64	GREAT BRITAIN
72	BELGIUM
74	HUNGARY
76	THE NETHERLANDS
84	ITALY
86	AZERBAIJAN
88	SINGAPORE
100	UNITED STATES
102	MEXICO
104	BRAZIL
116	LAS VEGAS
118	QATAR
120	ABU DHABI

108

FANS & FUTURE

108 2025 SEASON PREVIEW
Looking ahead to another thrilling championship this year

122 THE F1 FANDOM
How the sport has become more popular than ever

126 THE FUTURE OF F1
What advancements and changes could F1 see in the years to come?

36

INTRODUCTION

8 75 YEARS OF FORMULA 1
A brief history of the sport

14 THE EVOLUTION OF AN F1 CAR
Compare the vehicles of 1950 and today

22 INNOVATIONS
How F1 tech has made its way to road cars

26 BLUFFER'S GUIDE
New to F1? Here's what you need to know

CIRCUITS IN FOCUS

16	AUSTRALIA
18	CHINA
20	JAPAN
28	BAHRAIN
30	SAUDI ARABIA
32	MIAMI

75 YEARS OF FORMULA 1

As F1 celebrates a milestone anniversary in 2025, look back on its evolution with a brief history of the sport

Words Rob Clark

75 YEARS OF FORMULA 1

The very first motor race of the World Championship of Drivers – what we now call Formula 1 – took place at Silverstone in 1950. It was won by Giuseppe Farina, driving an Alfa Romeo, and Farina also went on to claim the inaugural title of world champion that year.

Thereafter, the 1950s were dominated by the great Juan Manuel Fangio, who won the drivers' title in 1951, and on four consecutive occasions from 1954-57. Acclaimed by Stirling Moss as "one of the greatest, if not the greatest, F1 driver of all time", to this day, Fangio's record of five world titles makes him the third most successful driver in the sport's history.

But while motor racing was new and exciting in the 1950s, it was also lethal. Two-time world champion Alberto Ascari was killed during testing at Monza in 1955, and that same year saw another tragedy at Le Mans when French driver Pierre Levegh and 83 spectators were killed. Remarkably the race continued, but the aftermath led to the withdrawal of Mercedes (the dominant marque at the time) from the sport. The team did not return to F1 for 40 years.

1950: At Silverstone, Giuseppe Farina in the Alfa Romeo 158 won the inaugural race of the first Drivers' World Championship.

75 YEARS OF FORMULA 1

Into the 60s, and little changed regarding driver safety, but the advent of the monocoque chassis and the introduction of Colin Chapman's Lotus 25/33 (probably the best car of the decade) firmly shifted the focus of F1 cars to their handling; arguably, it has remained the primary concern ever since. Improvements in suspension and aerodynamics also served to improve the cars' safety. The devastating death of Jim Clark, twice world champion, actually came during an F2 race, at Hockenheim.

Niki Lauda's two world titles (he added a third in 1984) and horrifying crash at the Nürburgring were arguably the central themes of F1 in the 1970s, highlighting both the talent and precarious existence of F1 drivers. It was a decade which also saw legendary figures such as Jackie Stewart, Emerson Fittipaldi, Jody Scheckter and, of course, James Hunt all claim world titles.

Hunt's playboy lifestyle and media-friendly persona led to a major uptick in interest in F1, and in 1978 TV started to show races in full. It just so happened that one of the main beneficiaries would be Hunt himself, who later proved to be as natural in the commentary box as he was on the track.

Graham Hill, another British two-time world champion (1962 and 1968), also won the Indy 500. When he won Le Mans in

> "WHILE MOTOR RACING WAS NEW AND EXCITING IN THE 1950S, IT WAS ALSO LETHAL"

1967: The 1960s saw the rise of the monocoque chassis, pioneered by Colin Chapman (right), and drivers such as Graham Hill (left) became popular public figures.

TIMELINE

1950
The World Drivers' Championship is introduced by governing body FIA (Federation Internationale de l'Automobile).

1957
Juan Manuel Fangio wins his fifth World Drivers' title at the age of 46.

75 YEARS OF FORMULA 1

1976: A problem with Niki Lauda's suspension at Nürburgring led to a terrible accident that left him with life-changing injuries.

1955: The damage to Alberto Ascari's Ferrari after the deadly crash at Monza.

1972, he became the first – and to date, only – driver ever to have achieved that remarkable hat trick. Significant regulation changes were also taking place: in 1973, Formula 1 saw the introduction of the safety car, while the formation lap and slick tyres also made their first appearances.

In 1974, Bernie Ecclestone co-founded the F1 Constructors' Association, becoming president four years later. He was to become a driving force behind TV deals, maximising revenue, improving safety and giving the F1 teams greater control over a range of matters. Sponsorship also arrived, in the form of tobacco giants JPS, Marlboro and Philip Morris.

The 1980s witnessed the rise of three all-time great drivers: Nelson Piquet (who won his three world titles in that decade), Alain Prost (who won three of his four) and Ayrton Senna (who won his first in 1989). As a result, rivalries developed and for almost the first time we saw these continue off the track as personalities clashed.

1962
The Lotus 25/33 designed by Colin Chapman is the first car to feature a monocoque chassis.

1975-77
Friends James Hunt and Niki Lauda dominate the middle part of the decade.

75 YEARS OF FORMULA 1

2024: The season's drivers posing for a portrait on the grid in Bahrain.

1986: Some of the sport's most successful drivers emerged in the 1980s, such as (left to right) Ayrton Senna, Alain Prost, Nigel Mansell and Nelson Piquet.

Late 70s – early 80s
The era of mass sponsorship begins, with tobacco companies coming to the fore.

1985-89
Alain Prost, 'the Professor' brings his meticulous approach to winning in 1985, '86 and '89.

1 May 1994
The death of Ayrton Senna at Imola prompted a revolution in the sport's approach to safety.

75 YEARS OF FORMULA 1

2000: Ferrari were a dominant force in F1 throughout the Noughties with the record-breaking Michael Schumacher behind the wheel.

2020: Thanks to continued efforts to improve safety, Romain Grosjean was able to walk away from a dramatic crash in Bahrain, escaping with minor burns.

And not just the drivers and teams, as Ecclestone and Max Mosley threatened a breakaway championship for which they later admitted they did not have the funding, but nevertheless left them in a stronger position.

As the 1990s arrived, the stunning Williams 14/14B car took Nigel Mansell to a well-deserved title in 1992, and Prost a year later (his last championship before retiring). Michael Schumacher went on to win the next two championships in the Benetton B194, which several drivers admitted was a "difficult" car to control.

But in 1994, tragedy struck. During qualifying for the San Marino Grand Prix at Imola, Austrian driver Roland Ratzenberger was killed. The following day Senna crashed and, like Ratzenberger, he died on impact. The reverberations were instant and significant. Immediately, tracks all over the globe had to be modified, and rules were brought in to slow the cars down. The rest of the decade focused on improving safety.

The first few years of the Noughties were all Schumacher as he won five consecutive titles (to add to the two he won in the 90s), from 2000-04. Car-wise, carbon fibre changed from being used in a few components to being the main material used in the chassis construction.

> "THE 2008 TITLE RACE WAS THE MOST DRAMATIC EVER – DECIDED IN THE LAST FEW SECONDS AND THE LAST FEW METRES"

The 2008 title race was the most dramatic ever – decided in the last few seconds and the last few metres. Hindsight has highlighted the importance of Lewis Hamilton clinching the title by the skin of his teeth having narrowly missed out the previous year. Although it would take Hamilton a further six years to add his second title, he has since become the joint most successful driver in F1 history.

The early 2010s were ruled by another German, Sebastian Vettel, who won in each of the first four years of the decade.

In 2011, F1 saw the introduction of DRS (Drag Reduction System), which could be deployed on certain sections of a track when a driver was within one second of the car in front. And in 2015 the halo cockpit protection system was brought in, a titanium framework around the drivers' heads which prevents them being hit by flying debris, a frequent cause of injury and even death in the early years of F1.

Following the Hamilton years, Max Verstappen took over and, driving the sensational Red Bull car, has won the last four world titles. There were signs, though, that his domination might be waning, and that this 75th year might yet see another of F1's famous shifts in the balance of power.

2004
Michael Schumacher wins his seventh World Championship to become the most successful driver of all time.

2 Nov 2008
At the Brazilian Grand Prix, the closest finish in F1 history sees Lewis Hamilton clinch his first title.

2023
The outstanding Red Bull car wins 21 out of 22 races, 19 of them for Max Verstappen.

THE EVOLUTION OF

Take a look at how much the technology and design of Formula 1 cars have changed from 1950 to today

Words Rob Clark

1. CHASSIS
THEN: The first Formula 1 cars featured a steel tubular frame and aluminium bodywork.
NOW: The cars use a monocoque design, made of carbon fibre, which is stiffer and allows for a lower frontal area.

2. SPEED
THEN: Early F1 cars could reach top speeds of around 290kph (180mph), and went from 0-100kph (60mph) in four seconds.
NOW: Top speeds can now exceed 354kph (220mph), and cars can accelerate from 0-100kph (60mph) in just two seconds. On average, a modern F1 car can decelerate from 100kph (60mph) to zero over just 15m (under 50ft).

3. BRAKES
THEN: Aluminium drum brakes were used, which were similar to road cars of the time.
NOW: Modern carbon brake discs can generate 5g of stopping force and withstand temperatures up to 1,000°C (1,832°F).

4. ENGINE
THEN: A 1.5-litre supercharged in-line eight-cylinder engine, which produced 350bhp.
NOW: A 1.6-litre V6 engine with a single turbocharger and two hybrid electric systems, which generates 1,000bhp.

5. GEARS
THEN: The cars used a traditional road car four-speed H-pattern gearbox with clutch, accelerator and brake pedals.
NOW: Modern F1 cars have eight gears, selected using paddles on the steering wheel. No clutch pedal.

THE EVOLUTION OF AN F1 CAR

AN F1 CAR

6 AERODYNAMICS AND DOWNFORCE

THEN: Besides a rudimentary streamlined chassis shape to help reduce drag, the advantages of aerodynamics and downforce were largely unknown in the 1950s.

NOW: The whole car's design is centred on aerodynamic efficiency, with sidepods and wings. Downforce is largely generated by airflow under the floor.

7 TYRES

THEN: Cars were fitted with skinny, grooved tyres, and used the same at both front and rear.

NOW: Tyres are now thicker, and can be 30% bigger at the rear than the front. Slicks increase cornering speed and acceleration, but also improve grip, leading to greater safety.

ALFA ROMEO 158 (1950)

MCLAREN MCL38 (2024)

8 STEERING WHEEL

THEN: These were made out of aluminium and wood, and had no other functions besides steering.

NOW: Now custom-built to suit each individual, drivers can change brake balance, engine settings, deploy DRS and speak to the team over the radio all from controls on the steering wheel.

9 SUSPENSION

THEN: Suspension was fairly simplistic, with transverse leaf springs at the front, and a swing axle at back.

NOW: Cars have a complex mix of springs, dampers, rockers, wishbones, pull and push rods, and axles. Suspension is now an integral aspect of aerodynamics and can change airflow around the car.

10 PROTECTION FOR DRIVERS

THEN: Drivers raced in a cloth cap and goggles, some even wore short-sleeved shirts. They sat upright and were largely unprotected.

NOW: Drivers use protective racewear and now sit much lower. The carbon fibre/Kevlar composite survival cell and halo system provide much greater protection in the event of a crash or flying debris.

AUSTRALIA

THE ALBERT PARK STREET CIRCUIT IN MELBOURNE IS A POPULAR OPENER TO THE GRAND PRIX SEASON

Albert Park, as the Australian Grand Prix venue is affectionately known, is a street circuit which uses normal roads in and around the public park after which it is named, with spectacular views of the Albert Park Lake and the Melbourne city skyline. Firmly established as the first race in the Grand Prix season, the track offers numerous opportunities for overtaking – not least on the long main straight which ends in a hairpin right-hand turn at the end – which makes for an exciting and dynamic race. Its first F1 race, in 1996, witnessed Michael Schumacher's debut win for Ferrari.

ALBERT PARK CIRCUIT

LOCATION	MELBOURNE, AUSTRALIA
FIRST GRAND PRIX	1996
CIRCUIT LENGTH	5.278KM (3.280MI)
NUMBER OF LAPS	58
RACE DISTANCE	306.124KM (190.217MI)
LAP RECORD	1:19.813 BY CHARLES LECLERC, 2024

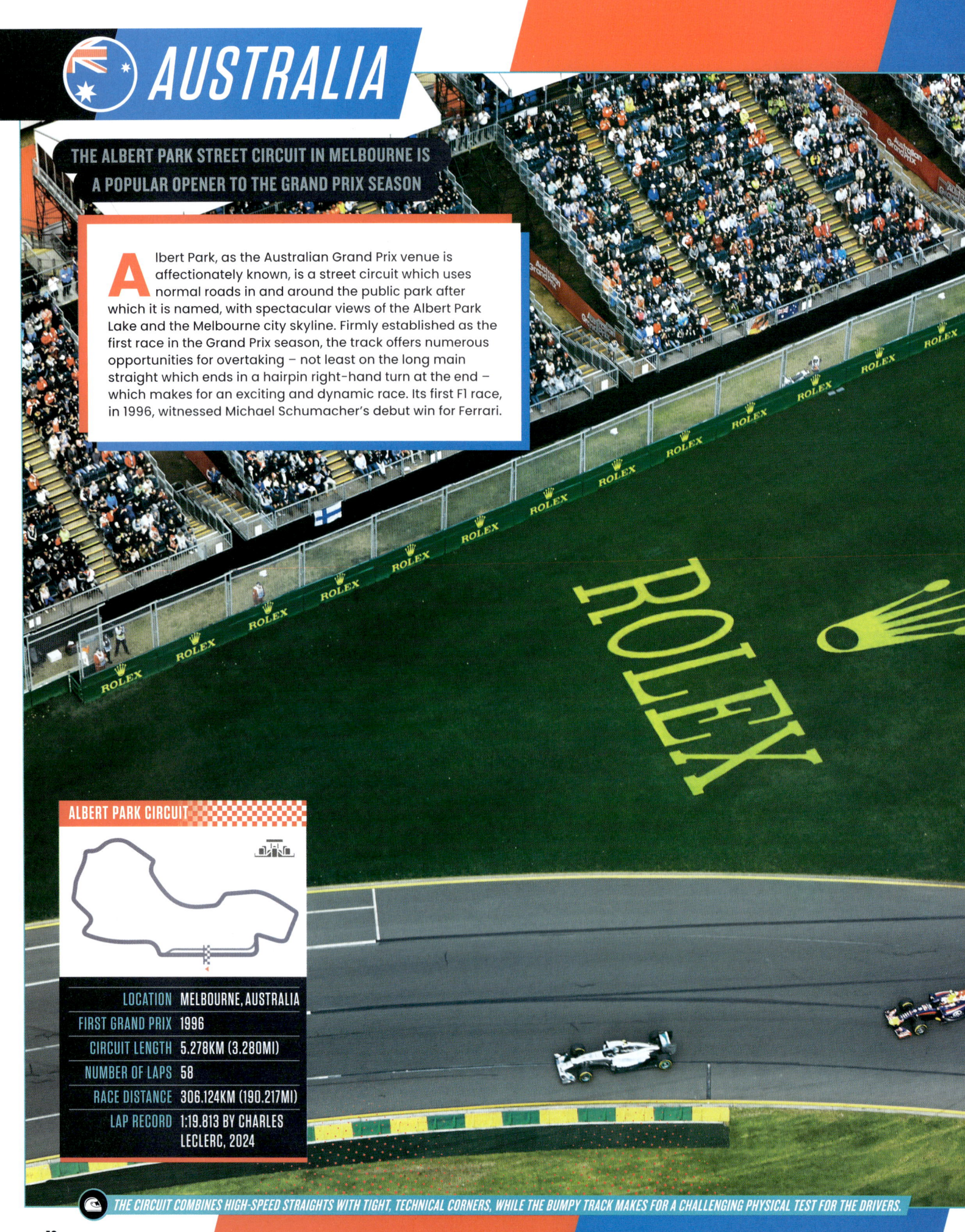

THE CIRCUIT COMBINES HIGH-SPEED STRAIGHTS WITH TIGHT, TECHNICAL CORNERS, WHILE THE BUMPY TRACK MAKES FOR A CHALLENGING PHYSICAL TEST FOR THE DRIVERS.

AUSTRALIA

HOST TO THE AUSTRALIAN GRAND PRIX SINCE 1996, THE ALBERT PARK CIRCUIT IS ONE OF THE LONGEST-RUNNING F1 VENUES.

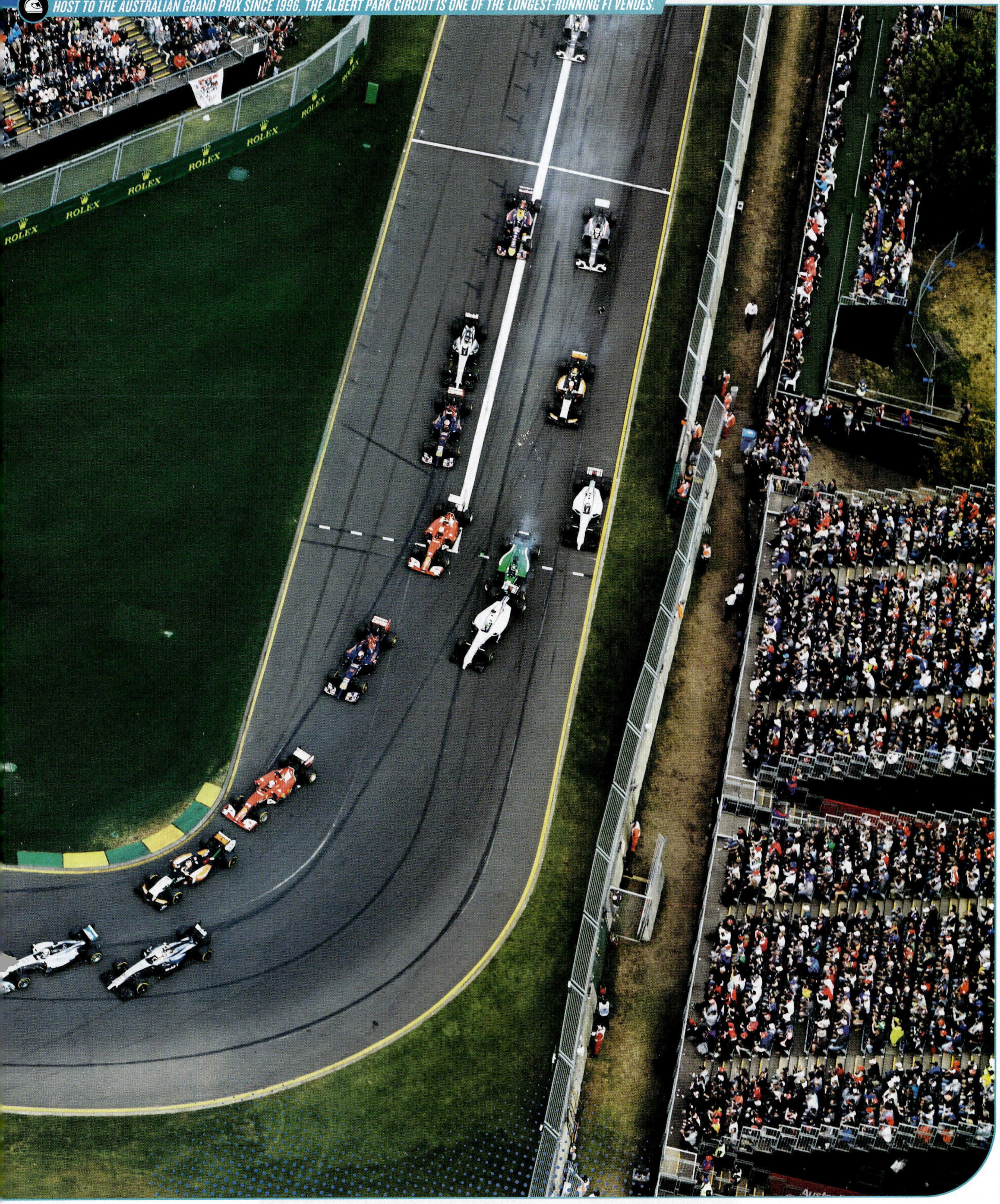

CHINA

A FIXTURE FOR THE PAST 20 YEARS, THE SHANGHAI INTERNATIONAL CIRCUIT HAS BROUGHT A NEW ELEMENT TO THE CALENDAR

Part of the Chinese government's ongoing desire to showcase the city to the world and establish that the nation is 'open to business', the Shanghai International Circuit was designed between April 2003 and April 2004 and purpose-built on former swampland in just 18 months. It opens spectacularly with ever-tightening Turns 1 and 2, while the super-high g-force Turns 7 and 8 provide a popular but challenging test for the drivers. As of the end of the 2024 season, there had been 17 F1 championships held at the circuit (racing was suspended from 2020 to 2023 due to the Covid pandemic) and Mercedes have won six of them, though Ferrari has more podium finishes.

THE CIRCUIT IS DESIGNED TO RESEMBLE THE CHINESE SYMBOL FOR 'SHANG' (MEANING 'UPWARDS') WHEN VIEWED FROM THE AIR.

CHINA

SHANGHAI FEATURES ONE OF THE LONGEST STRAIGHTS ON ANY F1 CIRCUIT IN THE WORLD – A 1.2KM (0.75MI) STRETCH BETWEEN TURNS 13 AND 14.

SHANGHAI INTERNATIONAL CIRCUIT

LOCATION	SHANGHAI, CHINA
FIRST GRAND PRIX	2004
CIRCUIT LENGTH	5.451KM (3.387MI)
NUMBER OF LAPS	56
RACE DISTANCE	305.066KM (189.559MI)
LAP RECORD	1:32.238 BY MICHAEL SCHUMACHER, 2004

🇯🇵 JAPAN

THE SUZUKA CIRCUIT IS A HIT WITH DRIVERS AND FANS ALIKE

From the off, Suzuka, as it is always called, was a firm favourite among the drivers. Fast and technically challenging, it is a figure-of-eight circuit set next to – and partly within – a giant funfair. The 'crossover' layout also maximises viewing opportunities for the fans and makes any seat a good one. The 130DR corner is acclaimed as a turn which asks questions of both a driver's skill and bravery; if the team gets the downforce configuration right, there are rare overtaking opportunities at the chicane immediately following the turn. Fernando Alonso audaciously went round the outside of Schumacher here in 2005.

AT SUZUKA, JULES BIANCHI SADLY BECAME THE MOST RECENT DRIVER (TO DATE) TO DIE IN AN F1 CRASH, AFTER HITTING A CRANE CLEARING THE WRECKAGE OF AN EARLIER INCIDENT.

JAPAN

AYRTON SENNA WON HIS FIRST F1 TITLE AT SUZUKA IN 1988. HE WAS INVOLVED IN CONTROVERSIAL INCIDENTS WITH ALAIN PROST IN EACH OF THE NEXT TWO YEARS AT THE CIRCUIT.

SUZUKA INTERNATIONAL RACING COURSE

LOCATION	SUZUKA, JAPAN
FIRST GRAND PRIX	1987
CIRCUIT LENGTH	5.807KM (3.608MI)
NUMBER OF LAPS	53
RACE DISTANCE	307.471KM (191.054MI)
LAP RECORD	1:30.983 BY LEWIS HAMILTON, 2019

F1 INNOVATIONS

You don't have to drive an F1 car to benefit from the sport's technology

Words David Smith

STEERING WHEEL BUTTONS

An F1 driver can't afford to take their eyes off the track to adjust a control, so ever since the 1970s more and more of the switches necessary to get peak performance out of a racing car have been placed on the steering wheel. The technology has jumped to road cars, but whereas you might be turning the radio up or setting your cruise control, an F1 driver will be adjusting brake bias or activating the DRS system.

F1 INNOVATIONS

KINETIC ENERGY RECOVERY SYSTEM

Part of F1's commitment to hybrid drivetrain technology, KERS allows a car to recover energy that would have been lost as heat when braking (F1 cars can also make use of heat from the turbocharger). This energy is then stored (either in a battery or a flywheel) and accessed when needed to give a boost to power output, helping to overtake or defend against overtaking. First introduced to F1 in 2009, it is now used on road cars as well. Hybrid and electric vehicles commonly use regenerative braking to charge their batteries, for example.

DIAMOND CYLINDER COATINGS

More accurately known as 'diamond-like' carbon (DLC) coatings, this innovation adds a thin layer of carbon-based material, very similar to diamonds, on the interior of a car's cylinders to reduce friction. The technology is now used on performance cars like the Ferrari 458 (pictured).

THE DOUBLE OVERHEAD CAMSHAFT

One of the first innovations to make it into mainstream cars, the DOHC was first used by Peugeot at the 1912 French Grand Prix (before the days of F1). The double camshaft allows an engine manufacturer to have four valves on each cylinder (one camshaft handling air intake and the other handling the exhaust), which improves airflow and boosts performance.

CARBON FIBRE CHASSIS

This lightweight – and incredibly strong – material was pioneered in the 19th century, and by the 1960s it was being used in engine parts by Rolls-Royce. It was first used in an F1 car in 1975, when Graham Hill used it in rear wing supports. In 1981, the McLaren racing team introduced the first ever carbon fibre chassis on an F1 car (the MP4/1 chassis). As well as being lighter, carbon fibre enhances safety thanks to its high stiffness-to-strength ratio, and the technology is now a feature of many high-performance cars, such as the McLaren 765LT (pictured above).

ACTIVE SUSPENSION

Changing the setup of your car to give either a smooth ride or a sportier one is achieved at the touch of a button these days, and that's all thanks to F1 technology. It was introduced in the 1980s, and by the early Nineties it was so good (Nigel Mansell won nine of 16 races in 1992 driving a Williams car with active suspension), that it was banned for the 1993 season.

F1 INNOVATIONS

PADDLE SHIFTERS

Surprisingly, this technology also goes all the way back to the turn of the 20th century, but it wasn't used in an F1 car until Ferrari introduced it in 1989. The semi-automatic system means the driver still decides when to make a gear change, but the wear and tear of a manual gearbox is avoided. Paddle shifters (often called 'flappy paddles') are now an option on many production cars, and typically come as standard on sports models.

ACTIVE AERODYNAMICS

The drag-reduction system (DRS) on an F1 car allows the driver to adjust the rear wing for enhanced aerodynamic properties, reducing drag and increasing speed. It is controversial, and is only allowed to be activated in specific circumstances – when within one second of the car in front, and even then only in specified zones on the circuit. It increases speed by allowing air to pass through the rear wing, and the technology can be found on high-performance road cars like the McLaren P1 (pictured above).

A BLUFFER'S GUIDE TO F1

New to Formula 1? Here's what you need to know to sound like an expert

Words David Smith

2024 drivers portrait

How many races are there in a season?

This varies – there were only seven in the first Formula 1 season back in 1950. In 2025, there will be 24 races (known as 'Grand Prix') and six sprints, stretching from 16 March to 7 December, taking place all around the world.

The Las Vegas Grand Prix, 2023

HOW MANY TEAMS ARE THERE?

Team numbers fluctuate as constructors enter and leave the sport (Ferrari are the only team to have competed in every year of Formula 1 since 1950). In 2025 there will be ten teams, each entering two cars on each race weekend. As well as their two drivers, teams also carry reserve drivers who can step in if needed.

A BLUFFER'S GUIDE TO F1

Perez, Verstappen and Alonso on the podium in Miami, 2023

Starting grid at Silverstone, 2023

HOW DOES THE POINTS SYSTEM WORK?

The winning driver of a Grand Prix earns 25 championship points, with the second-placed driver taking 18. The following places get 15, 12, 10, 8, 6, 4, 2 and 1 point. Identical points are awarded to the constructors of each car for their own championship.

What does a race weekend involve?

This is different for weekends when there is a sprint (there will be six sprints in 2025). On regular weekends, teams get to practise on Fridays, then record timed laps during qualifying on the Saturday. The fastest cars are then placed at the top of the starting grid for the Grand Prix on Sunday. On sprint weekends, some of the practice sessions are replaced by sprint qualifying and the sprint itself on the Saturday, with Grand Prix qualifying taking place after the sprint. The Grand Prix then follows as usual on the Sunday.

Valtteri Bottas in Azerbaijan, 2016

Shanghai sprint, 2024

How fast are the cars?

The fastest speed ever clocked in qualifying or a race was 378kph (235mph), by Valtteri Bottas in Azerbaijan in 2016. The fastest average speed over a full race was 247.6kph (153.8mph), set by Michael Schumacher in 2003, when driving a Ferrari in the Italian Grand Prix at Monza.

WHAT ARE SPRINTS?

Sprint weekends were added to the F1 calendar in 2021 and give fans an extra chance to see their favourite drivers in competitive action. Taking place over a shorter distance (100km/62mi), these fast and furious races take place on the Saturday before the main Grand Prix. Points are awarded to the top eight drivers (from eight points down to one) and count towards both the drivers' and constructors' championships.

 BAHRAIN

THE BAHRAIN GRAND PRIX IS NOW ONE OF FOUR TO BE HELD IN THE MIDDLE EAST

Sakhir is often windy, and teams can experience a wide range of fluctuating temperatures, leading to tricky race conditions. On the other hand, these also lead to exciting races and a fair amount of overtaking. The highlight section is the tight, left-hand downhill Turn 10 (pictured), though the speed at which the drivers can take Turn 12 is something many of them enjoy. Lewis Hamilton holds the record of five race wins on the circuit, which didn't start life as a night race – it switched to that in 2014 to celebrate the race's tenth anniversary. In 2020, two rounds of the F1 championship took place on the circuit, to increase the number of races during a Covid-hit season.

BAHRAIN INTERNATIONAL CIRCUIT

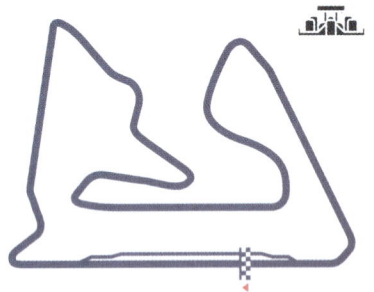

LOCATION	SAKHIR, BAHRAIN
FIRST GRAND PRIX	2004
CIRCUIT LENGTH	5.412KM (3.363MI)
NUMBER OF LAPS	57
RACE DISTANCE	308.238KM (191.530MI)
LAP RECORD	1:31.447 BY PEDRO DE LA ROSA, 2005

THE FIRST F1 RACE ON THE SAKHIR CIRCUIT TOOK PLACE ON 4 APRIL 2004 AND WAS THE FIRST F1 GRAND PRIX TO BE HELD IN THE MIDDLE EAST.

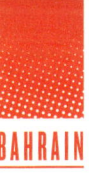

THE BAHRAIN GRAND PRIX MADE THE HEADLINES IN 2020 WHEN FRENCH DRIVER ROMAIN GROSJEAN MIRACULOUSLY ESCAPED A FIREBALL CRASH WHICH LOOKED LIKELY TO BE FATAL.

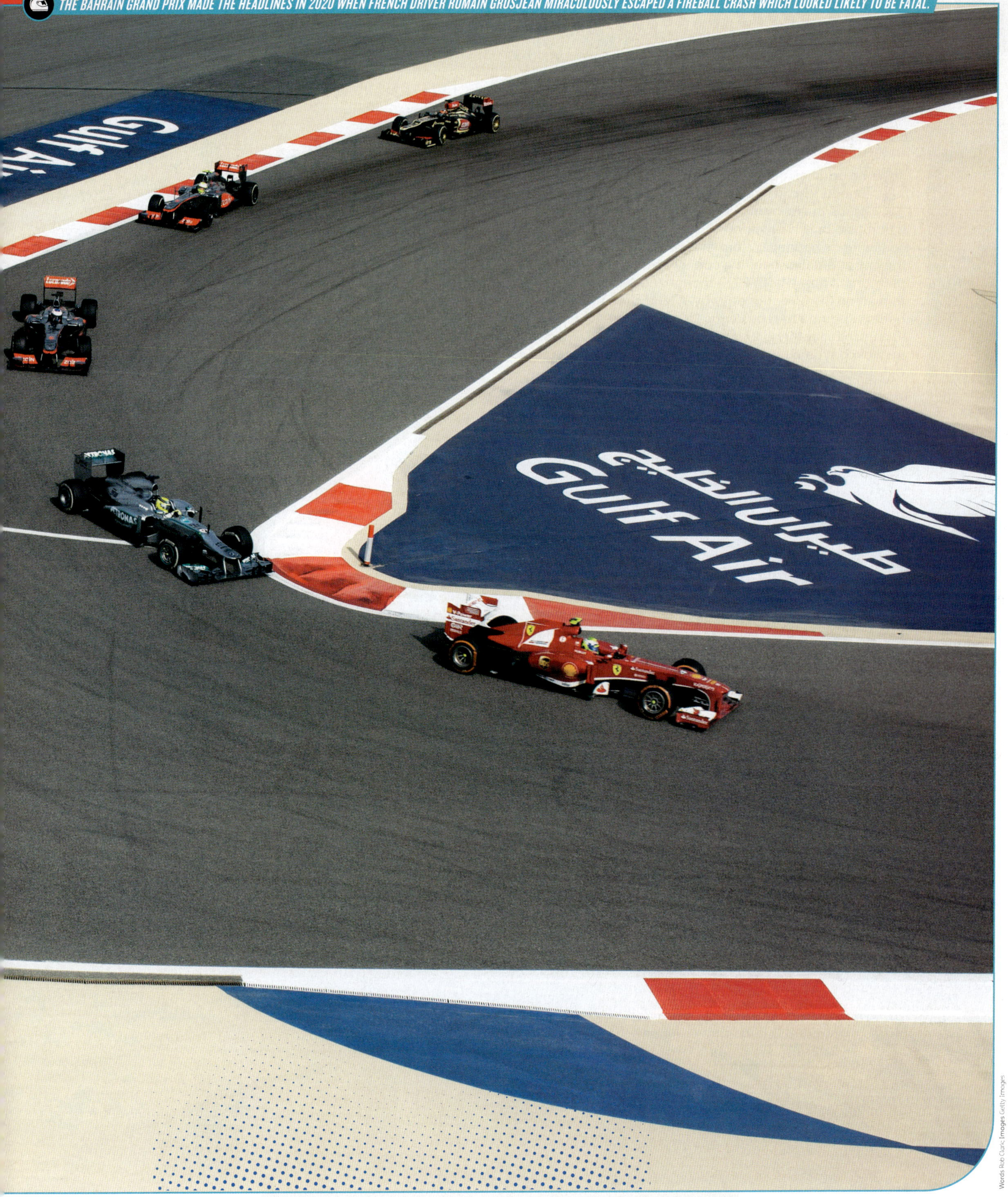

Words Rob Clark; Images Getty Images

SAUDI ARABIA

THE LONG, FAST TRACK AT JEDDAH IS AN INTERESTING ADDITION TO THE F1 CALENDAR

The addition of a Saudi Arabian Grand Prix was announced in late 2020, with the inaugural race taking place the following year at Jeddah. It is expected that a purpose-built motorsports complex – the brainchild of a consultancy headed by former F1 driver Alexander Wurz – in the city of Qiddiya, near the capital Riyadh, will become a more permanent home from 2027, though the Jeddah circuit might remain on the calendar anyway. A long circuit (third longest, behind Spa and the Las Vegas Strip), the Jeddah track is also fast despite featuring 27 corners. The race takes place at night to avoid daytime temperatures that can reach 35 degrees Celsius (95 degrees Fahrenheit).

THE PLAN FOR THE NEW SAUDI ARABIAN CIRCUIT IN QIDDIYA INCLUDES A TURN WITH ELEVATION AS HIGH AS A 20-STOREY BUILDING. IT HAS BEEN DUBBED 'THE BLADE'.

SAUDI ARABIA

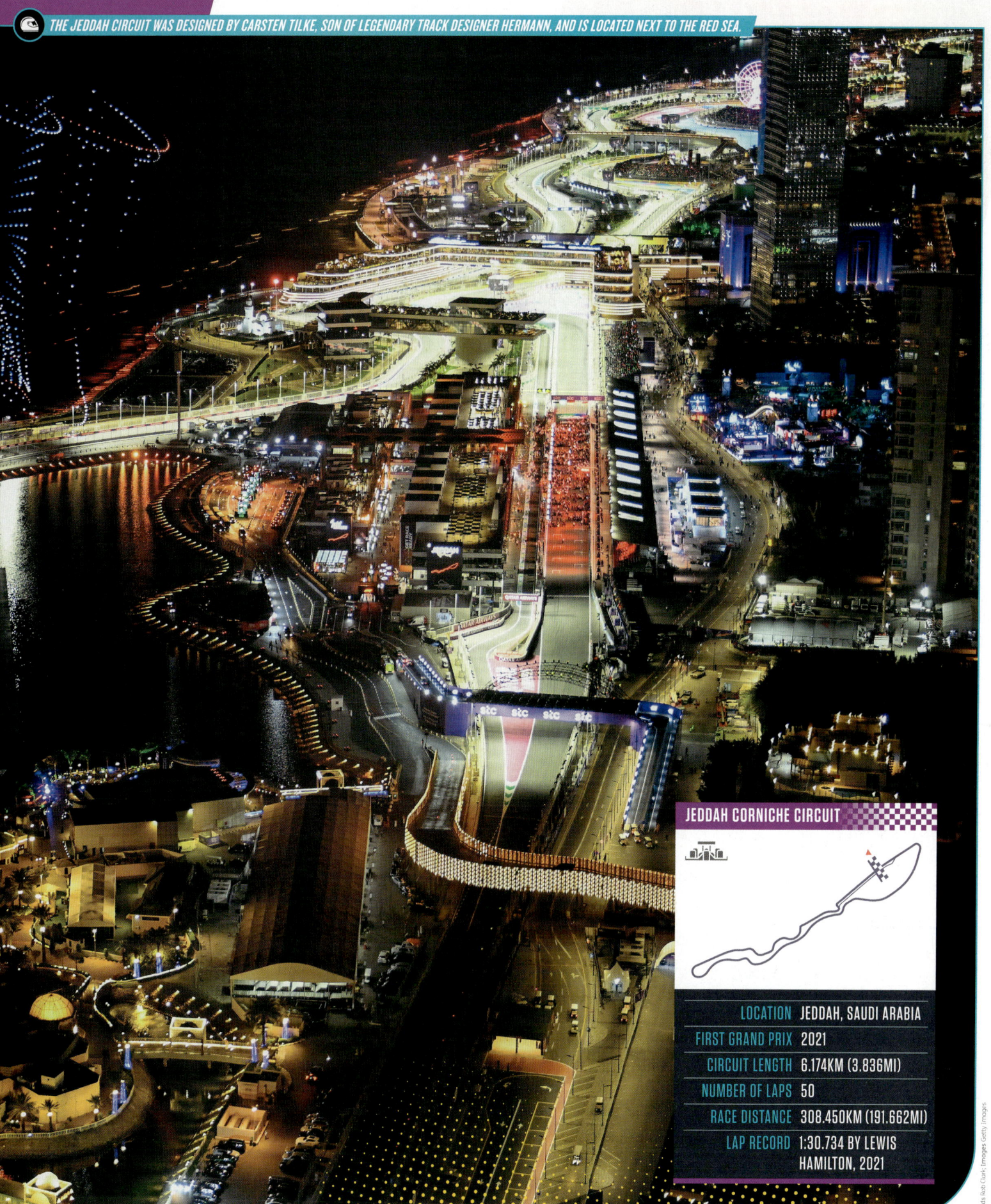

THE JEDDAH CIRCUIT WAS DESIGNED BY CARSTEN TILKE, SON OF LEGENDARY TRACK DESIGNER HERMANN, AND IS LOCATED NEXT TO THE RED SEA.

JEDDAH CORNICHE CIRCUIT

LOCATION	JEDDAH, SAUDI ARABIA
FIRST GRAND PRIX	2021
CIRCUIT LENGTH	6.174KM (3.836MI)
NUMBER OF LAPS	50
RACE DISTANCE	308.450KM (191.662MI)
LAP RECORD	1:30.734 BY LEWIS HAMILTON, 2021

MIAMI

F1'S NEWEST CIRCUIT HAS ALL THE ATTRIBUTES TO BECOME A DRIVER AND FAN FAVOURITE

The Miami International Autodrome is a temporary structure, but that's easy to forget as there is a permanent feel to it. It has a street circuit vibe similar to that of Melbourne's Albert Park, but is actually set in the same Hard Rock Stadium complex which houses the NFL's famous Miami Dolphins team. Stadium owner Stephen Ross had long harboured a desire to host a Grand Prix. Unsurprisingly, no overall F1 records have been set on the circuit yet, but it is smooth (the track is not used for any other motorsports events in between Grand Prix races) and quick, so braking and picking the right racing line are important elements.

IN THE THREE F1 RACES TO TAKE PLACE IN MIAMI SO FAR (AS OF 2024), NO DRIVER HAS WON THE RACE FROM POLE POSITION.

MIAMI

IT WAS ON THE MIAMI CIRCUIT IN 2024 THAT BRITISH DRIVER LANDO NORRIS CLAIMED HIS MAIDEN F1 VICTORY.

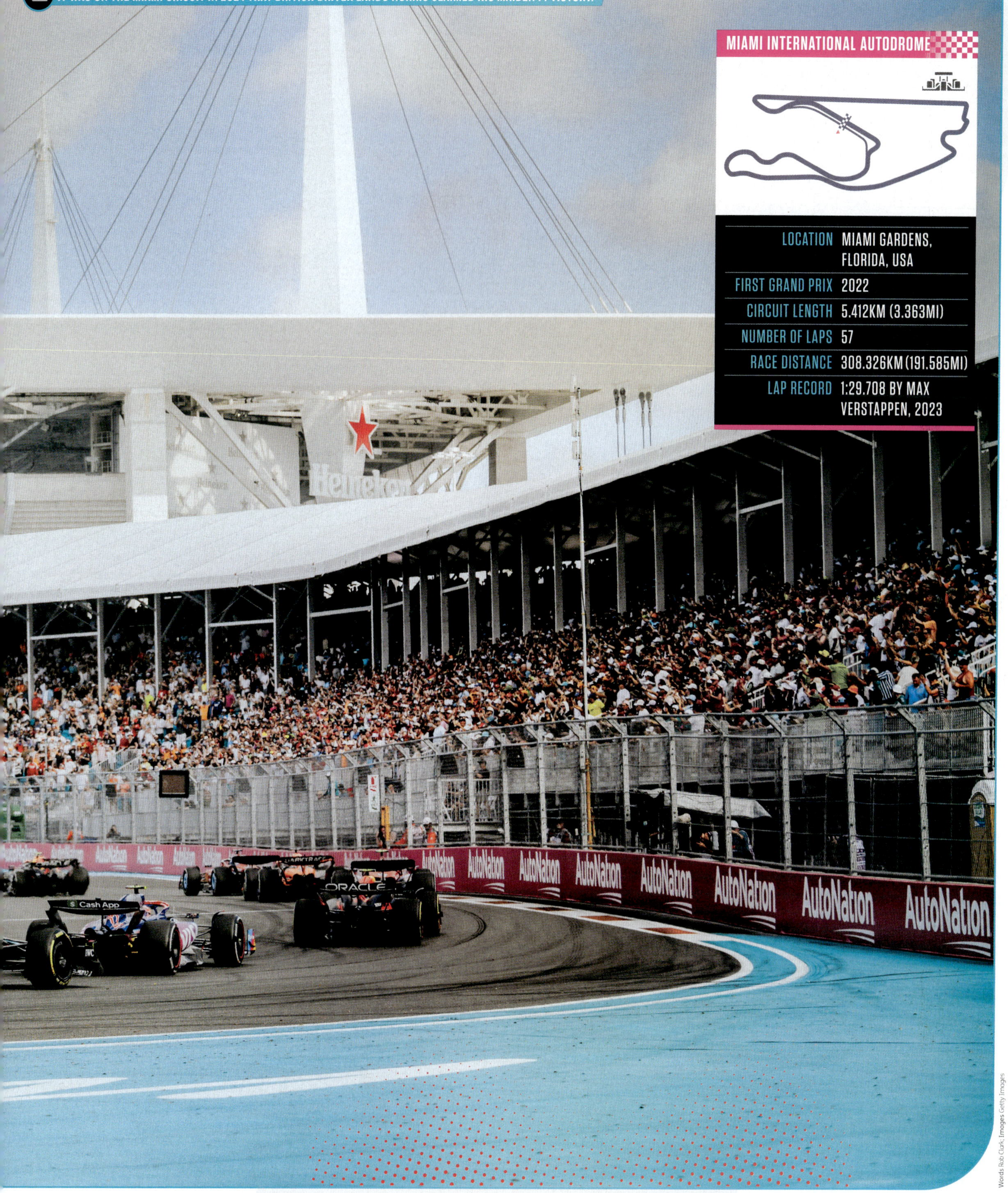

MIAMI INTERNATIONAL AUTODROME

LOCATION	MIAMI GARDENS, FLORIDA, USA
FIRST GRAND PRIX	2022
CIRCUIT LENGTH	5.412KM (3.363MI)
NUMBER OF LAPS	57
RACE DISTANCE	308.326KM (191.585MI)
LAP RECORD	1:29.708 BY MAX VERSTAPPEN, 2023

TEAMS & DRIVERS

36 MEET THE TEAMS
An introduction to the ten constructors

52 HALL OF FAME
Get to know some of the most successful drivers in the sport's history

56 DRIVER TRAINING
How drivers prepare for the intense physical challenges of a race

66 TEAM TACTICS
The strategies behind race success

70 PIT STOPS
How engineers perform ultra-fast stops

78 RIVALRIES
From friendly competition to driver drama

90 2024 SEASON REVIEW
How the previous championship unfolded

CIRCUITS IN FOCUS

46	IMOLA	76	THE NETHERLANDS
48	MONACO	84	ITALY
50	SPAIN	86	AZERBAIJAN
60	CANADA	88	SINGAPORE
62	AUSTRIA	100	UNITED STATES
64	GREAT BRITAIN	102	MEXICO
72	BELGIUM	104	BRAZIL
74	HUNGARY		

MEET THE TEAMS

Enter the high-tech garages of the ten constructors on the Formula 1 grid

Words Scott Reeves

Alpine

Although Alpine are based in rural Oxfordshire, they bring a splash of French flair to the grid courtesy of parent company, Renault. Officially, they are relative newcomers, but Alpine are just the latest of several iterations. Originally established as Toleman in 1981, the team rebranded as Benetton in 1986, Renault in 2002, Lotus in 2012 and Renault again in 2015, before settling on Alpine (after Renault's sports car subsidiary) in 2021. That debut season saw the team's greatest success to date when Esteban Ocon was a surprise victor at the Hungarian Grand Prix. Although Alpine have remained a middle-of-the-grid outfit, the team has significant resources at its disposal thanks to Renault's technological expertise and a cadre of big-name investors, including actor Ryan Reynolds, NFL superstar Patrick Mahomes, golfer Rory McIlroy and footballer Juan Mata. However, 2025 will be Alpine's final season using Renault power units before they begin buying Mercedes engines in 2026. Perhaps another rebrand is on the cards?

TEAM HISTORY

Toleman (1981-85) ➔ Benetton (1986-2001) ➔ Renault (2002-2011) ➔ Lotus (2012-2015) ➔ Renault (2016-2020) ➔ Alpine (2021-Present)

Alpine celebrating two podium places in Brazil, 2024.

Full name: BWT Alpine F1 Team
Based in: Enstone, Oxfordshire, UK
Total race wins: 1
Total fastest laps: 1
Total pole positions: 0
Total podiums: 6
Total Constructors' Championship wins: 0
Total Drivers' Championship wins: 0

MEET THE TEAMS

Full name: Aston Martin Aramco F1 Team
Based in: Silverstone, Northamptonshire, UK
Total race wins: 0
Total fastest laps: 3
Total pole positions: 0
Total podiums: 9
Total Constructors' Championship wins: 0
Total Drivers' Championship wins: 0

Aston Martin

Aston Martin's early foray into Formula 1 didn't bring much success. The team entered a handful of races in 1959 and 1960 and didn't win a single point before calling it quits. They returned in 2021, however, when Canadian billionaire Lawrence Stroll invested in the Aston Martin company and rebranded his Racing Point F1 team with Aston Martin's classic green livery. Stroll has made significant investments to improve his team's infrastructure and personnel. He's built a state-of-the-art factory directly opposite Silverstone. He's agreed a new deal with Honda for engines that'll kick in at the start of the 2026 season. He's also recruited top-tier talent, including former champions Sebastian Vettel and Fernando Alonso, but Stroll has also been accused of nepotism since his son Lance has a spot on the team locked in. Aston Martin are currently the best of the midfield teams on the grid and are often in the fight for a place on the podium, but Stroll's lofty ambition is that Aston Martin will soon be challenging for championship titles.

Aston Martin mechanics at work, 2024.

TEAM HISTORY

Aston Martin (1959-1960)

Jordan (1991-2005) → Midland (2006) → Spyker (2007) → Force India (2008-2018) → Racing Point (2019-2020) → Aston Martin (2021-Present)

MEET THE TEAMS

Full name: Scuderia Ferrari HP
First entry: 1950
Based in: Maranello, Italy
Total race wins: 248
Total fastest laps: 263
Total pole positions: 253
Total podiums: 826
Total Constructors' Championship wins: 16
Total Drivers' Championship wins: 15

Ferrari

No team has a more storied history in Formula 1 than Ferrari. Their iconic red cars ('rosso corsa' to use the exact colour) are instantly recognisable, having competed in every Formula 1 season since the sport was inaugurated in 1950. Given Ferrari's long association with F1, it should come as no surprise that they're also the sport's most successful team. Ferrari have won the Constructors' Championship 16 times, seven ahead of their nearest rivals. Ferrari drivers have lifted the Drivers' Championship 15 times, with notable winners including Michael Schumacher, Sebastian Vettel and Juan Manuel Fangio. It isn't just Enzo Ferrari's successors at Maranello who expect success. The team's passionate fans, known as the Tifosi, follow their chosen team around the world and show a passion and dedication that's unmatched by any other team's fans. They haven't had much to cheer of late, however, since the last driver to win the championship in Ferrari colours was Kimi Räikkönen in 2007.

Ferrari team portrait, 2024.

TEAM HISTORY

Ferrari (1950–Present)

MEET THE TEAMS

Haas

America is the market that Formula 1 would love to crack, but it faces stiff competition from NASCAR and IndyCar. That hasn't stopped American industrialist Gene Haas setting up the first American-led team in Formula 1 since the 1980s. Most independent constructors purchase engines from one of the established manufacturers, but Haas did things a little differently. They entered a close partnership with Ferrari that allows them not just to use the Italian company's engines, but to benefit from extra technical support. Haas have also taken on Ferrari's junior drivers like Mick Schumacher and Antonio Giovinazzi, giving them a first taste of F1 racing. The relationship has raised eyebrows around the paddock since many insiders regard Haas to be little more than a Ferrari testing ground, but if Haas do have an unfair advantage compared to their independent rivals, it hasn't translated into better results. Haas finished bottom of the pile in 2023, and the embarrassing 2021 season saw them fail to clinch a single point.

TEAM HISTORY

Haas (2016-Present)

Haas team portrait, 2016.

Full name: *MoneyGram Haas F1 Team*
Based in: *Kannapolis, North Carolina, USA*
Total race wins: *0*
Total fastest laps: *3*
Total pole positions: *1*
Total podiums: *0*
Total Constructors' Championship wins: *0*
Total Drivers' Championship wins: *0*

MEET THE TEAMS

McLaren

McLaren were originally formed for selfish reasons. In 1963, F1 driver Bruce McLaren couldn't find a team willing to provide a car for him to race in a lower-level motorsport championship, so he made his own. The experiment was a success, and three years later, McLaren debuted a car in Formula 1. In the years since, McLaren have become one of the most successful F1 teams. It reached a peak in the late 1980s and early 1990s when McLaren engineers gained a reputation for innovation, and Alain Prost and Ayrton Senna each won the Drivers' Championship three times in McLaren's iconic white-and-red cars. In recent years, McLaren have struggled to maintain relevance and looked set to glide towards the back of the grid alongside its old rival Williams. However, the team has re-emerged as a force with Lando Norris and Oscar Piastri at the wheel and McLaren won their first Constructors' Championship for 26 years in 2024.

McLaren celebrating their 2024 Constructors' Championship win.

TEAM HISTORY

McLaren (1966-Present)

Full name: McLaren Formula 1 Team
Based in: Woking, Surrey, UK
Total race wins: 189
Total fastest laps: 172
Total pole positions: 164
Total podiums: 523
Total Constructors' Championship wins: 9
Total Drivers' Championship wins: 12

MEET THE TEAMS

Full name: Mercedes-AMG Petronas F1 Team
Based in: Brackley, Northamptonshire, UK
Total race wins: 129
Total fastest laps: 109
Total pole positions: 142
Total podiums: 298
Total Constructors' Championship wins: 8
Total Drivers' Championship wins: 9

Mercedes

German luxury car maker Mercedes were one of the biggest names in Formula 1 during the sport's earliest years, and Juan Manuel Fangio won consecutive Drivers' Championships while driving for the team in 1954 and 1955. However, the team withdrew from F1 at the end of the second championship year, partly due to a tragic accident at Le Mans that killed Mercedes driver Pierre Levegh and 83 spectators. Mercedes didn't return until 2010, when they purchased the Brawn GP team. It didn't take long for the team to hit the headlines. They persuaded German national hero Michael Schumacher to come out of retirement, then Schumacher made way for another uber-talented driver. Lewis Hamilton arrived just as a new-spec Mercedes engine proved to be superior to anything else on offer, and he teamed up with Nico Rosberg and Valtteri Bottas to win eight consecutive Constructors' Championships. Though the Silver Arrows have struggled since 2021, there's no doubt that the Brackley-based German outfit know how to win as they transition to a future without Lewis Hamilton.

Hamilton bade farewell to Mercedes after the 2024 season.

TEAM HISTORY

Mercedes (1954-1955)

Tyrrell (1970-1998) → **BAR** (1999-2005) → **Honda** (2006-2008) → **Brawn GP** (2009) → **Mercedes** (2010-Present)

MEET THE TEAMS

Full name: Visa Cash App Racing Bulls Formula One Team
Based in: Faenza, Italy
Total race wins: 0
Total fastest laps: 1
Total pole positions: 0
Total podiums: 0
Total Constructors' Championship wins: 0
Total Drivers' Championship wins: 0

Racing Bulls

A year after dipping their toe into Formula 1, the Red Bull drinks company bought struggling Minardi, a team that had never emerged as a force during their 21 years on the grid. Red Bull rebranded the team as Toro Rosso (Italian for Red Bull) and used them as a junior team. They were subsequently renamed AlphaTauri (after Red Bull's fashion brand) and are now Racing Bulls. Although they run as a separate outfit to the senior Red Bull racing team, Racing Bulls have been a training ground for teams in the Red Bull driver development programme. Among the drivers who got their first start in one of the team's cars are Max Verstappen, Carlos Sainz Jr, Pierre Gasly and Alex Albon. Racing Bulls are set to continue as a conveyor belt of talent, with the bigger teams eagerly watching each new cohort of drivers to see if they have what it takes to succeed in the competitive world of Formula 1.

RB team portrait, 2024.

TEAM HISTORY

Minardi (1985-2005) ➡ **Toro Rosso** (2006-2019) ➡ **AlphaTauri** (2020-2023) ➡ **RB** (2024) ➡ **Racing Bulls** (2025-Present)

MEET THE TEAMS

Red Bull

When the Jaguar F1 team was put up for sale in 2004, energy drink manufacturer Red Bull leapt at the chance to buy it. The top tier of motorsport was the ideal theatre to market their brand, which was associated with high-adrenaline adventure and extreme sports. The team leaned on veteran David Coulthard at first, but soon developed a reputation for fostering young talent from within. That approach paid dividends when Sebastian Vettel won four consecutive Drivers' Championship titles at the start of the 2010s, and it worked a second time when Max Verstappen won another four in a row to open the 2020s. A big part of Red Bull's success was down to chief designer Adrian Newey, who Red Bull plucked from McLaren for their first venture into Formula 1. Newey has recently moved on to pastures new, but team principal Christian Horner is still with the team, as he has been since its inception.

Red Bull team members pose in the garage at Abu Dhabi, 2024.

TEAM HISTORY

Stewart (1997-1999) ➡ **Jaguar** (2000-2004) ➡ **Red Bull** (2005-Present)

Full name: Oracle Red Bull Racing
Based in: Milton Keynes, Buckinghamshire, UK
Total race wins: 122
Total fastest laps: 99
Total pole positions: 103
Total podiums: 282
Total Constructors' Championship wins: 6
Total Drivers' Championship wins: 8

MEET THE TEAMS

Kick Sauber

Sauber have been a mainstay on the Formula 1 grid for more than three decades, having started life under Swiss motorsport executive Peter Sauber in 1993. Sauber tried everything to make his private team competitive, trying out self-built engines and purchasing power units from Mercedes, Ford, BMW and Ferrari. The team's best moments came under BMW, when they finished second and third in the 2007 and 2008 Constructors' Championships. The 2008 campaign also saw Robert Kubica claim Sauber's solitary race win at the Canadian Grand Prix, with teammate Nick Heidfeld finishing second. Sauber's current deal is with Ferrari, although 2025 will be the last season they work together. After that, the team will take to the grid as a rebranded Audi F1 team. Sauber have a reputation for blooding talented young drivers like Felipe Massa, Kimi Räikkönen, Sebastian Vettel and Charles Leclerc, often placing them alongside veterans at the tail end of their career.

Sauber CEO and CTO Mattia Binotto (left) with team members, 2024.

TEAM HISTORY

Sauber (1993-2005) → **BMW Sauber (2006-2009)** → **Sauber (2010-2018)** → **Alfa Romeo (2019-2023)** → **Kick Sauber (2024-2025)** → **Audi (2026 onward)**

Full name: Stake F1 Team Kick Sauber
Based in: Hinwil, Zurich, Switzerland
Total race wins: 1
Total fastest laps: 3
Total pole positions: 0
Total podiums: 10
Total Constructors' Championship wins: 0
Total Drivers' Championship wins: 0

MEET THE TEAMS

Full name: Williams Racing
Based in: Grove, Oxfordshire, UK
Total race wins: 114
Total fastest laps: 133
Total pole positions: 128
Total podiums: 312
Total Constructors' Championship wins: 9
Total Drivers' Championship wins: 7

Williams

Williams were the brainchild of former driver and mechanic Frank Williams, who formed a Formula 1 team with engineer Patrick Head in 1977. They were a great combination, and it didn't take long for their cars to reach the front of the pack. The team's glory years came in the 1980s and 1990s with nine Constructors' Championships and seven Drivers' Championships (each won by a different driver). Williams had to battle through adversity, however. Frank Williams suffered a road traffic accident in 1986 that left him in a wheelchair for the rest of his life, although he remained team principal for another 34 years. The team then suffered a tragic loss on the racetrack in 1994, when Ayrton Senna had a fatal accident at Imola. Williams were sold to investors in 2020, and Frank Williams finally stepped away from the team with which he'd become the most successful independent constructor in Formula 1 history. The golden era of Williams now seems to be in the rear-view mirror, but they're still a big name on the F1 grid.

Williams team portrait, 2017.

TEAM HISTORY

- **Williams** (1978-Present)

IMOLA

IMOLA HAS BEEN THE SCENE FOR SOME GREAT RACES, AND SOME AWFUL TRAGEDIES

Imola, or to give it its full name, the Emilia-Romagna Grand Prix, is a thrill ride from start to finish. The anti-clockwise layout is fast, with iconic turns such as Acque Minerali and Piratella which can be taken quickly, but it also rewards drivers who stay on the track – or at least penalises those who don't, as the presence of grass and gravel deters drivers from going too wide at many of the corners. There are also elevation changes and a beautiful hilly backdrop which only add to the charm. In 2025, which is currently the last contracted visit to Imola, it will once again mark F1's first visit of the season to Europe.

IMOLA WAS THE CIRCUIT WHERE AYRTON SENNA AND ROLAND RATZENBURGER BOTH SADLY LOST THEIR LIVES ON CONSECUTIVE DAYS IN 1994.

IMOLA

THE 2023 RACE WAS CANCELLED TWO DAYS BEFORE THE RACE WEEKEND BEGAN AS STORM MINERVA HAD CAUSED WIDESPREAD FLOODING IN THE REGION.

AUTODROMO INTERNAZIONALE ENZO E DINO FERRARI

LOCATION	IMOLA, ITALY
FIRST GRAND PRIX	1980
CIRCUIT LENGTH	4.909KM (3.050MI)
NUMBER OF LAPS	63
RACE DISTANCE	309.049KM (192.034MI)
LAP RECORD	1:15.484 BY LEWIS HAMILTON, 2020

MONACO

THE CIRCUIT MAY LACK EXCITEMENT, BUT THE RACE NEVER DOES

The narrow, iconic street circuit offers few passing opportunities – so much so that three-time world champion Nelson Piquet once likened it to "riding a bicycle around your living room". Nevertheless its challenge is so unique that drivers love the circuit anyway, considering it a true drivers' track because of its twists and turns and the mental concentration required from start to finish. Being run on normal streets, the track is very narrow and cambered. In contrast to the tight, precise nature of the racing, away from the track race weekend is one long party with millionaires' boats moored up in the harbour around which the race is run.

CHARLES LECLERC'S VICTORY IN 2024 WAS THE FIRST BY A MONEGASQUE (NATIVE OF MONACO) SINCE LOUIS CHIRON WON THE MONACO GRAND PRIX IN 1931, 93 YEARS EARLIER.

THE MONACO GRAND PRIX HAS BEEN AN EVER-PRESENT ON THE F1 WORLD CHAMPIONSHIP CALENDAR SINCE 1955.

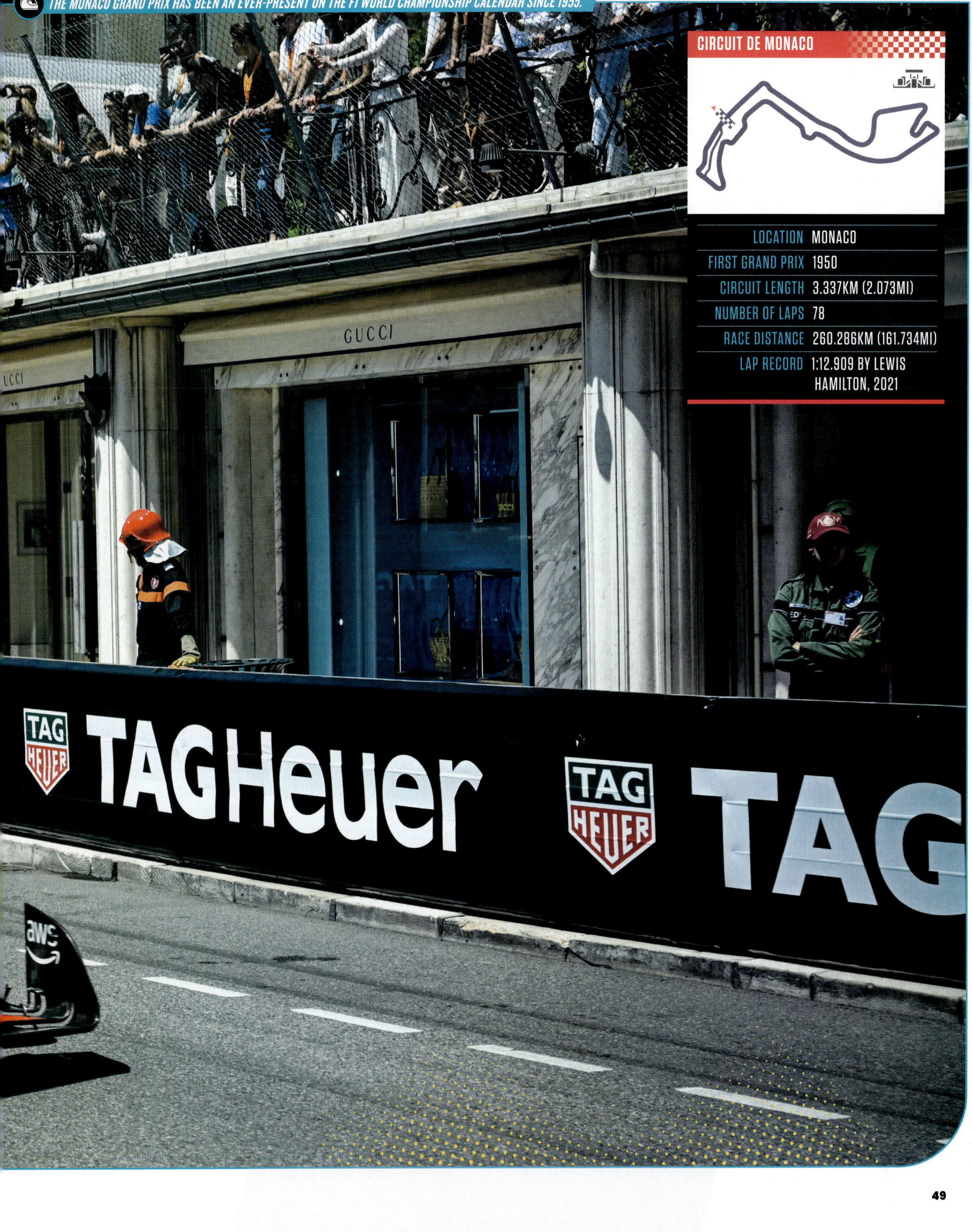

CIRCUIT DE MONACO

LOCATION	MONACO
FIRST GRAND PRIX	1950
CIRCUIT LENGTH	3.337KM (2.073MI)
NUMBER OF LAPS	78
RACE DISTANCE	260.286KM (161.734MI)
LAP RECORD	1:12.909 BY LEWIS HAMILTON, 2021

Words Rob Clark; Images Getty Images

SPAIN

THE SPANISH GRAND PRIX IS A POPULAR ONE WITH THE DRIVERS

Built as part of the sporting development programme for the 1992 Olympic Games, the Barcelona-Catalunya Circuit was first used for the Spanish Grand Prix in 1991. It had a spectacular start to life too, as Nigel Mansell and Ayrton Senna battled down the straight alongside each other before Mansell won out and went on to claim the race victory. The track offers an enticing mix of high- and low-speed corners, giving it a flow which is particularly physically demanding for the drivers. The tarmac is quite tough on tyres, and overtaking opportunities are not plentiful, so pit stop strategy is a crucial factor.

IT'S JUST AS WELL THAT DRIVERS DO ENJOY THE BARCELONA CIRCUIT, AS IT IS TRADITIONALLY USED REGULARLY FOR WINTER TESTING.

SPAIN

IN 34 RACES (AS OF 2024), THERE HAVE BEEN ONLY TEN OCCASIONS WHERE THE DRIVER STARTING FROM POLE HAS NOT GONE ON TO WIN THE RACE HERE.

CIRCUIT DE BARCELONA-CATALUNYA

LOCATION	BARCELONA, SPAIN
FIRST GRAND PRIX	1991
CIRCUIT LENGTH	4.657KM (2.894MI)
NUMBER OF LAPS	66
RACE DISTANCE	307.236KM (190.907MI)
LAP RECORD	1:16.330 BY MAX VERSTAPPEN, 2023

HALL OF FAME

Meet some of the most successful drivers in the history of Formula 1

Words Scott Reeves

Lewis Hamilton
2007-Present

Hamilton graduated from the McLaren Young Driver Programme and made an immediate impression in 2007, missing out on the Drivers' Championship by a single point in the most impressive rookie season F1 has seen. The margin between first and second was one point again in 2008, but this time Hamilton was the driver on the top of the podium. He added six more titles in seven years after a surprise move to Mercedes in 2013 to take advantage of the German constructor's dominant engine, before joining Ferrari in 2025.

- 7 Drivers' Championships
- Most race wins (105)
- Most pole positions (104)

Niki Lauda
1971-1979, 1982-1985

Lauda was on course to defend the Drivers' Championship he'd won in 1975 when a horror crash and fire at the 1976 German Grand Prix almost ended his life. Despite being given the last rites by a priest, Lauda rallied and was back on the grid in his Ferrari just six weeks later. He regained the Drivers' Championship crown in 1977 and added a third with McLaren in 1984 by just half a point, but it was Lauda's bravery and determination to finish second in 1976 that he'll always be remembered for.

- 3 Drivers' Championships
- 54 podium finishes
- Closest Drivers' Championship winning margin

HALL OF FAME

Juan Manuel Fangio
1950-1951, 1953-1958

The first superstar of F1, Fangio holds several records that will likely never be bettered. He won 24 of his 51 races and claimed five Drivers' Championships with four different teams. He excelled in longer races thanks to his unrivalled stamina, and he could wrestle the steering wheel for lap after lap in an era before power steering. He even missed a non-championship race in 1958 after being kidnapped by Cuban revolutionaries, but was thankfully released after 29 hours.

- 5 Drivers' Championships
- Highest win percentage (47.06%)
- Oldest Drivers' Champion (46y, 41d)

Sebastian Vettel
2007-2022

Vettel served an 18-month apprenticeship at Toro Rosso before being promoted to Red Bull, and he immediately repaid the faith shown in him by team bosses. He outscored his more experienced teammate Mark Webber to finish second in the Drivers' Championship before an amazing run of four consecutive titles between 2010 and 2013. The 2010 and 2012 titles went down to the last race of the season, but the other two were dominant displays in which Vettel finished more than 100 points ahead of his nearest rival.

- 4 Drivers' Championships
- Most pole positions in a single season (15)
- Youngest Drivers' Champion (23y, 134d)

Alain Prost
1980-1991, 1993

Prost had a smooth, relaxed driving style and his intellectual approach to racing saw him dubbed 'the Professor', but that didn't stop him falling out with Ayrton Senna, his teammate of two years at McLaren. The rivalry came to a head in the last race of 1989 when the two teammates collided on the track, a result that handed Prost his third Drivers' Championship. After a one-season sabbatical in 1992, Prost returned for a final fling with Williams that saw him become a four-time champion.

- 4 Drivers' Championships
- 51 race wins
- 41 fastest laps

HALL OF FAME

Ayrton Senna
1984–1994

Three Drivers' Championships seems too few for such a brilliant driver, a genius behind the wheel who sought to shave every tiny fraction of a second he could off his lap times. Perhaps there would have been more, but Senna died at the wheel of his Williams at the 1994 San Marino Grand Prix. Before then, he'd enjoyed a sensational debut season despite driving an uncompetitive Toleman, he'd outdriven three different teammates at Lotus, and he'd famously battled with Alain Prost at McLaren.

- 3 Drivers' Championships
- 65 pole positions
- Most Monaco Grand Prix wins (6)

Michael Schumacher
1991–2006, 2010–2012

Schumacher won two Drivers' Championships with Benetton in 1994 and 1995 before adding five on the trot with Ferrari from 2000 to 2004. At times he was unstoppable. He finished on the podium in all 17 races of the 2002 season, and in 2004 he won 13 of 18 races to secure the Drivers' Championship by a colossal margin. Schumacher was supremely fit, drove consistently on the limit for lap after lap, and gave mechanics detailed reports on how his car handled.

- 7 Drivers' Championships
- Most fastest laps (77)
- Most consecutive Drivers' Championships (5)

Jackie Stewart
1965–1973

Stewart finished top of the pile in 1969, 1971 and 1973 to join the sport's elite as a treble champion, but his greatest legacy had nothing to do with his 27 race wins. Instead, Stewart left his mark by being a tireless campaigner to improve safety at tracks. He pushed for the adoption of safety barriers, seatbelts, run-off areas and full-face helmets, and chose not to compete at his final Grand Prix after the death of his teammate François Cevert in qualifying.

- 3 Drivers' Championships
- 27 race wins
- 43 podium finishes

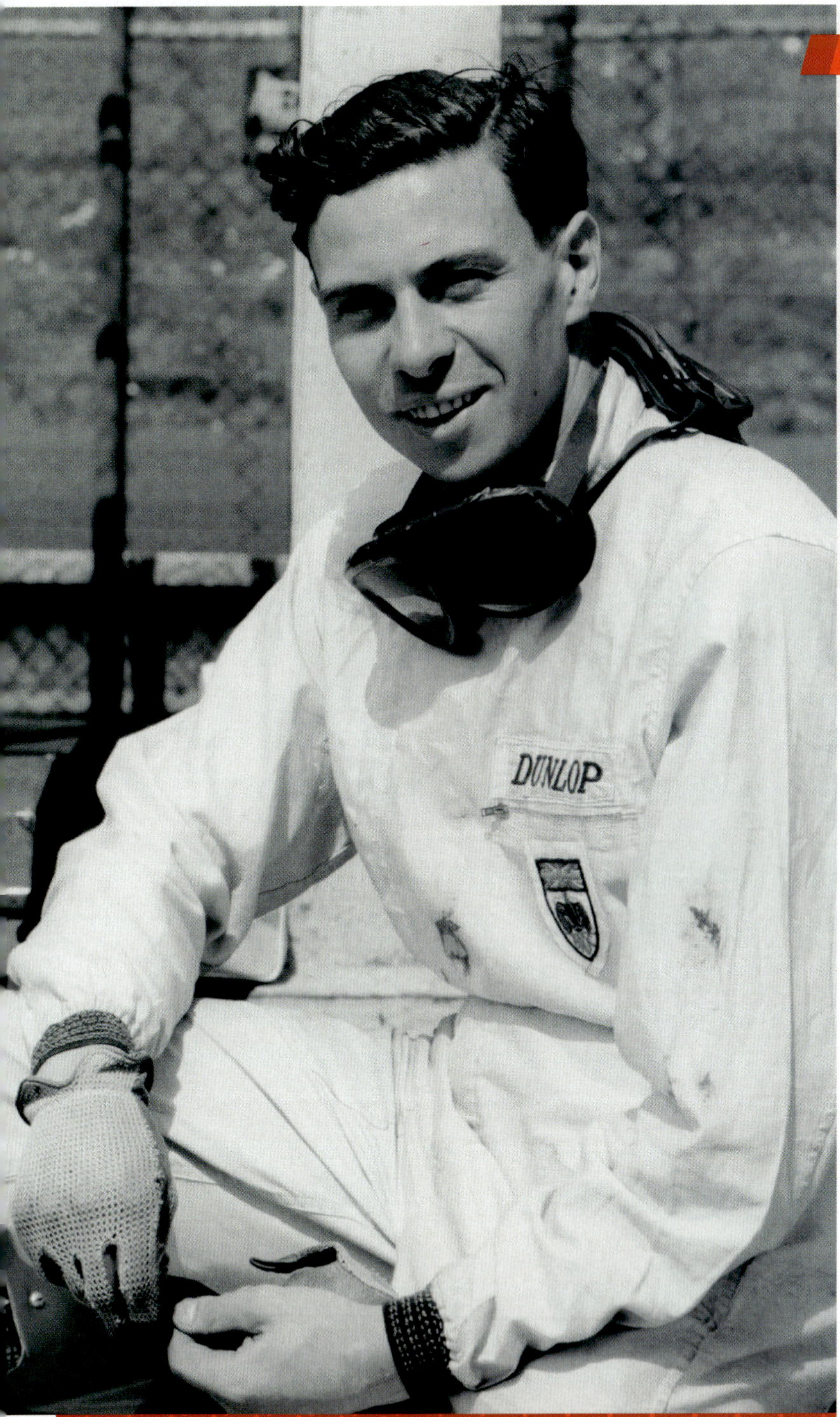

Jim Clark

1960–1968

Clark won the Drivers' Championship for the first time in a peerless 1963 campaign that saw him win seven of ten races, and he regained the title in 1965 after engine failure denied him the honour in 1964. A quiet and shy man in a grid of extroverts, Clark was nevertheless confident in his abilities and came into his own in difficult driving conditions. He was leading the 1968 Drivers' Championship when he was killed in a Formula 2 crash, an accident that robbed the motorsport of one of its greatest natural talents.

- *2 Drivers' Championships*
- *34.72% win percentage*
- *25 race wins*

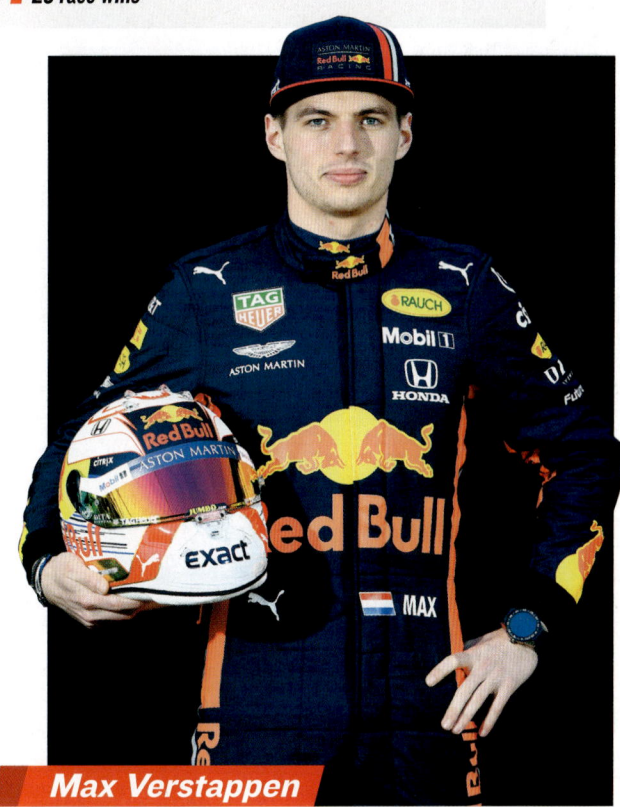

Max Verstappen

2015–Present

Verstappen was tipped as a future world champion almost as soon as he made his debut as the youngest ever F1 driver in 2015. It took him until 2021 to take the Drivers' Championship, and it was a combative campaign with a controversial finish to the last race. There was no questioning the next three years, however, when Verstappen was way ahead of the competition. In 2023, he won ten races in a row and 19 out of 22 races in total, the most dominant single season ever seen in F1.

- *4 Drivers' Championships*
- *Most consecutive race wins (10)*
- *Most race wins in a single season (19)*

DID YOU KNOW: AS OF 2024, ONLY JIM CLARK, SEBASTIAN VETTEL AND MAX VERSTAPPEN HAVE EACH ACHIEVED GRAND SLAMS* IN THREE CONSECUTIVE YEARS

Images Getty Images, Alamy. Stats and records correct as of January 2025.
*A Grand Slam is achieved if, in the same weekend, a driver: has pole position, the fastest lap, leads every lap and wins the race.

FIT TO DRIVE

How Formula 1 drivers prepare for the rigours of the season

Words David Smith

It would be easy to imagine that the cars are doing all the work during a Grand Prix, but the drivers are being subjected to immense physical and mental stresses as they push their machines, and their bodies, to the limit.

As cars have become quicker and more powerful, the strain placed on drivers has increased. Cockpit temperatures can reach well in excess of 38°C (100°F), while the g-forces that come with rapid acceleration and high-speed cornering are brutal. Add in the fact that the race will normally take around 90 minutes to complete, and a remarkable combination of strength and endurance is required.

F1 drivers are already a special breed – requiring excellent reflexes, a fierce competitive spirit, an ability to focus for long periods and the single-minded determination to achieve their goal. To complete a season of 24 races, plus practices, qualifying and sprints, F1 drivers also need to be in peak physical condition, and the process of attaining that splits into pre-season and in-season phases.

▶

A great deal of mental resilience is required for drivers to maintain their focus under stressful and physically demanding conditions.

Pre-season preparation

Drivers have roughly three months from the end of one season to the start of the next. Some downtime is essential, but this is also the period where they will lay the groundwork for their next campaign, building their cardio fitness back up after a long and gruelling season.

Cardio fitness focuses on 'zone 2' aerobic performance, where the body is functioning at between 60 and 70 per cent of its full capacity. Running and cycling are the usual methods of achieving this – the drivers do not push themselves to the limit, but concentrate on building stamina. Shorter bursts of high-intensity aerobic activity are then mixed in – faster runs that get a driver's heart rate close to its maximum level for brief periods.

While cardio training continues, a driver will move on to strength work. Overall body strength, especially core strength, is important, but particular attention is paid to the neck, which must support the head (and the weight of the helmet) through multiple turns at up to five times the force of gravity. It is calculated that the neck of an F1 driver has to support 34kg (75lb) of weight, over and over again, for corner after corner. To prepare, the neck is exercised from all directions, with loads of up to 80kg (176lb) to build strength and endurance.

Another strain on a driver's body (which most viewers would never anticipate) is that applied through braking. A driver has to apply tremendous pressure to the brake pedal to slow his vehicle down on the approach to a corner, often while applying subtle touches to the accelerator. This imbalance, with each side of the body under very different stresses, requires a rock-solid core if pain and injury are to be avoided.

An often overlooked key component of pre-season training is nutrition. Drivers are thoroughly tested to identify any deficiencies in their nutrition, which can then be addressed through diet and supplements.

In-season preparation

Maintaining fitness is the key once a season starts. A lot of the training done in pre-season is no longer necessary –

F1 simulators allow drivers to practise away from the track, helping them refresh their memory of a circuit's layout before the race.

Above and right: Pierre Gasly performs a warm-up exercise to test his reactions before a race.

FIT TO DRIVE

It's important for drivers to rehydrate after races – they can lose several kilos of water weight through sweat.

Drivers must maintain excellent physical fitness to withstand the g-forces experienced when driving at such high speeds.

> "PARTICULAR ATTENTION IS PAID TO TRAINING THE NECK, WHICH MUST SUPPORT THE HEAD THROUGH MULTIPLE TURNS AT UP TO FIVE TIMES THE FORCE OF GRAVITY"

Drivers use resistance apparatus to help train their neck muscles and warm up before races.

the season itself is so gruelling it will do part of the job of keeping fitness and strength levels steady, so fewer cardio and strength-training workouts are needed.

Recovery is also of critical importance, with the day after a race usually reserved for stretching and making sure no minor injuries (which could turn into major injuries if overlooked) have been picked up.

Nutrition remains critical during the long season as well. Drivers need to eat a diet rich in proteins and complex carbohydrates. Grilled fish and lean meats, along with vegetables and grains, are the staples. The emphasis is on a simple diet, because a bout of indigestion during qualifying or (even worse) a race could seriously impair a driver's focus and performance.

And as soon as a race is over, preparation begins for the next one. A carefully balanced drink will be in a driver's hand within half an hour of completing a grand prix, replacing the fluids and minerals lost during the ordeal just endured, and starting to prepare for the one to come.

 CANADA

THE CANADIAN GRAND PRIX CIRCUIT BEARS THE NAME OF THE COUNTRY'S MOST FAMOUS DRIVER

The fast, low-downforce circuit in Montreal is liked by the drivers because of its stop-start nature involving lots of chicanes, which require heavy braking. At the end of the lap is the iconic Wall of Champions – so called because Jacques Villeneuve, Michael Schumacher and Damon Hill all detoured into it in the same year. The circuit's origins lie in the creation of man-made Notre Dame Island, built in the middle of the St Lawrence River to host the 1967 Expo 67 World's Fair. Nine years later, the 1976 Montreal Olympic Games used the island, and after that, it became the permanent home to the Canadian Grand Prix. Initially, it was called the Circuit Ile Notre-Dame, but was renamed Circuit Gilles Villeneuve in the Canadian driver's honour.

THE FIRST GRAND PRIX HELD ON THE CIRCUIT WAS WON BY CANADIAN DRIVER GILLES VILLENEUVE. THE COURSE WAS RENAMED AFTER HIM FOLLOWING HIS DEATH IN 1982.

CANADA

> IN 1969, AL PEASE BECAME THE ONLY F1 DRIVER TO BE DISQUALIFIED FOR DRIVING TOO SLOWLY. PEASE HAD COMPLETED JUST 22 LAPS WHEN THE LEADERS HAD FINISHED ON 46.

CIRCUIT GILLES VILLENEUVE

LOCATION	MONTREAL, CANADA
FIRST GRAND PRIX	1978
CIRCUIT LENGTH	4.361KM (2.709MI)
NUMBER OF LAPS	70
RACE DISTANCE	305.27KM (189.68MI)
LAP RECORD	1:13.078 BY VALTTERI BOTTAS, 2019

AUSTRIA

NAME CHANGES AND REMODELLING HAVE NOT STOPPED THE CIRCUIT FROM BEING A POPULAR ONE

Starting out as the Österreichring (itself a replacement for the Zeltweg airfield circuit), the Austrian track gained a fearsome reputation for its fast, flowing curves which were dangerous for the cars of the time, due to their lack of downforce and grip compared to today. The circuit was dropped from the calendar in 1988, but legendary designer Hermann Tilke re-fashioned it and the A1-Ring, as it was then known, was back in action in 1997. Though much shorter than it was, the A1-Ring still packed a punch with the power required for the uphill first half, while the second half featured a series of quick, downhill corners. Rebuilt again, the circuit, now the Red Bull Ring, reopened to F1 in 2014.

RED BULL OWNER DIETRICH MATESCHITZ BOUGHT THE TRACK IN 2004, BUT IT TOOK A DECADE BEFORE IT WAS ONCE AGAIN ADDED TO THE F1 ROSTER.

AUSTRIA

IN 1975, STORMY WEATHER CUT THE RACE TO 29 LAPS (HALF-POINTS WERE AWARDED) AND WINNER VITTORIO BRAMBILA 'CELEBRATED' BY PROMPTLY CRASHING INTO A WALL.

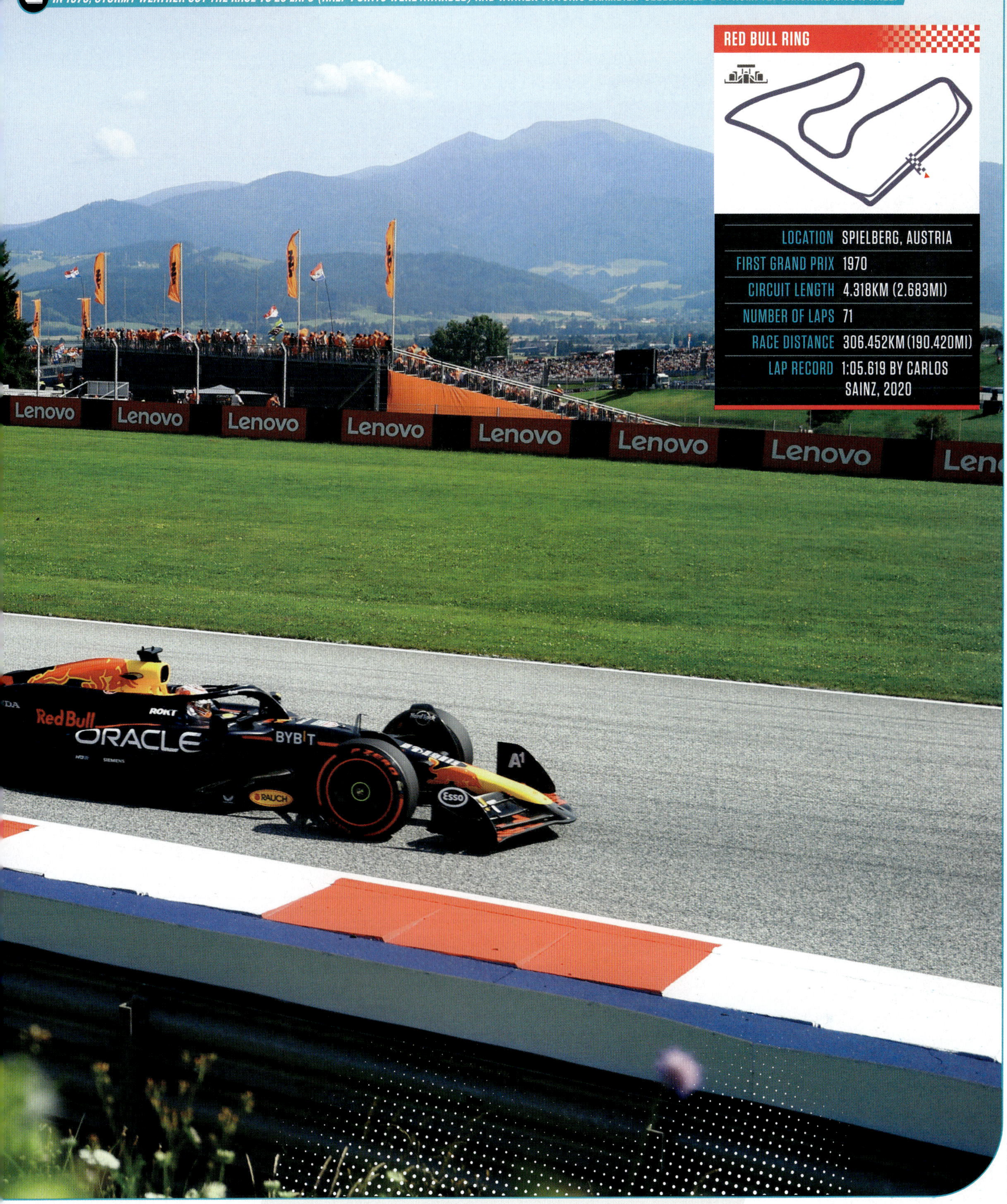

RED BULL RING

LOCATION	SPIELBERG, AUSTRIA
FIRST GRAND PRIX	1970
CIRCUIT LENGTH	4.318KM (2.683MI)
NUMBER OF LAPS	71
RACE DISTANCE	306.452KM (190.420MI)
LAP RECORD	1:05.619 BY CARLOS SAINZ, 2020

GREAT BRITAIN

SILVERSTONE IS THE FIRST – AND LAST – WORD IN HIGH-SPEED EXCITEMENT

Drivers love Silverstone. It's a circuit where high-tech F1 cars really come into their own, using downforce to manoeuvre through the high-speed corners and experience an adrenaline rush like nowhere else. Numerous layout changes since its 1950 debut have done nothing to slow the Silverstone track down. Former world champions Lewis Hamilton, Jenson Button and Jacques Villeneuve have all described Copse as one of the best corners anywhere in F1. "Flat out and hardcore," said Hamilton, who has won the race a record nine times. "You need to have serious confidence in yourself and the car. You're going 190mph [305kph] when you arrive, and you can't see much." The Hangar Straight, Becketts Corner and Stowe Corner are all renowned within the global motorsports community.

SILVERSTONE CIRCUIT

LOCATION	SILVERSTONE, UK
FIRST GRAND PRIX	1950
CIRCUIT LENGTH	5.891KM (3.660MI)
NUMBER OF LAPS	52
RACE DISTANCE	306.198KM (190.263MI)
LAP RECORD	1:27.097 BY MAX VERSTAPPEN, 2020

SILVERSTONE HOSTED THE FIRST-EVER F1 WORLD CHAMPIONSHIP ROUND ON 13 MAY 1950. GIUSEPPE FARINA WON IN AN ALFA ROMEO AND LATER TOOK THE TITLE.

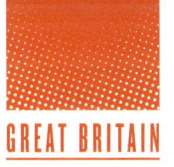

THE 1951 RACE AT SILVERSTONE SAW THE FIRST GRAND PRIX WIN FOR THE MOST SUCCESSFUL F1 CAR MARQUE IN HISTORY – FERRARI.

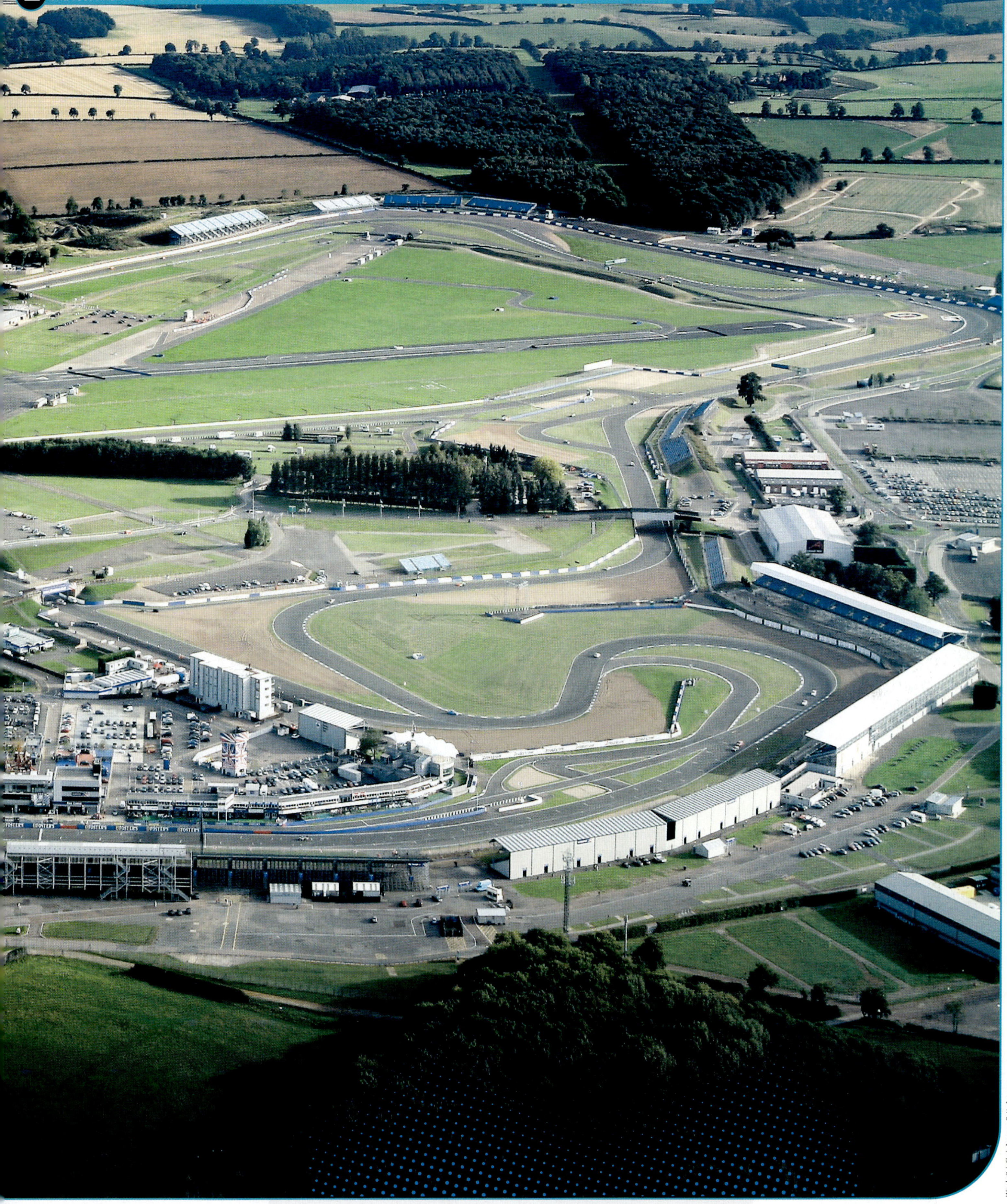

Words Rob Clark, Images Getty Images

The Ferrari team prepare for a race start simulation during winter testing in Spain, 2018.

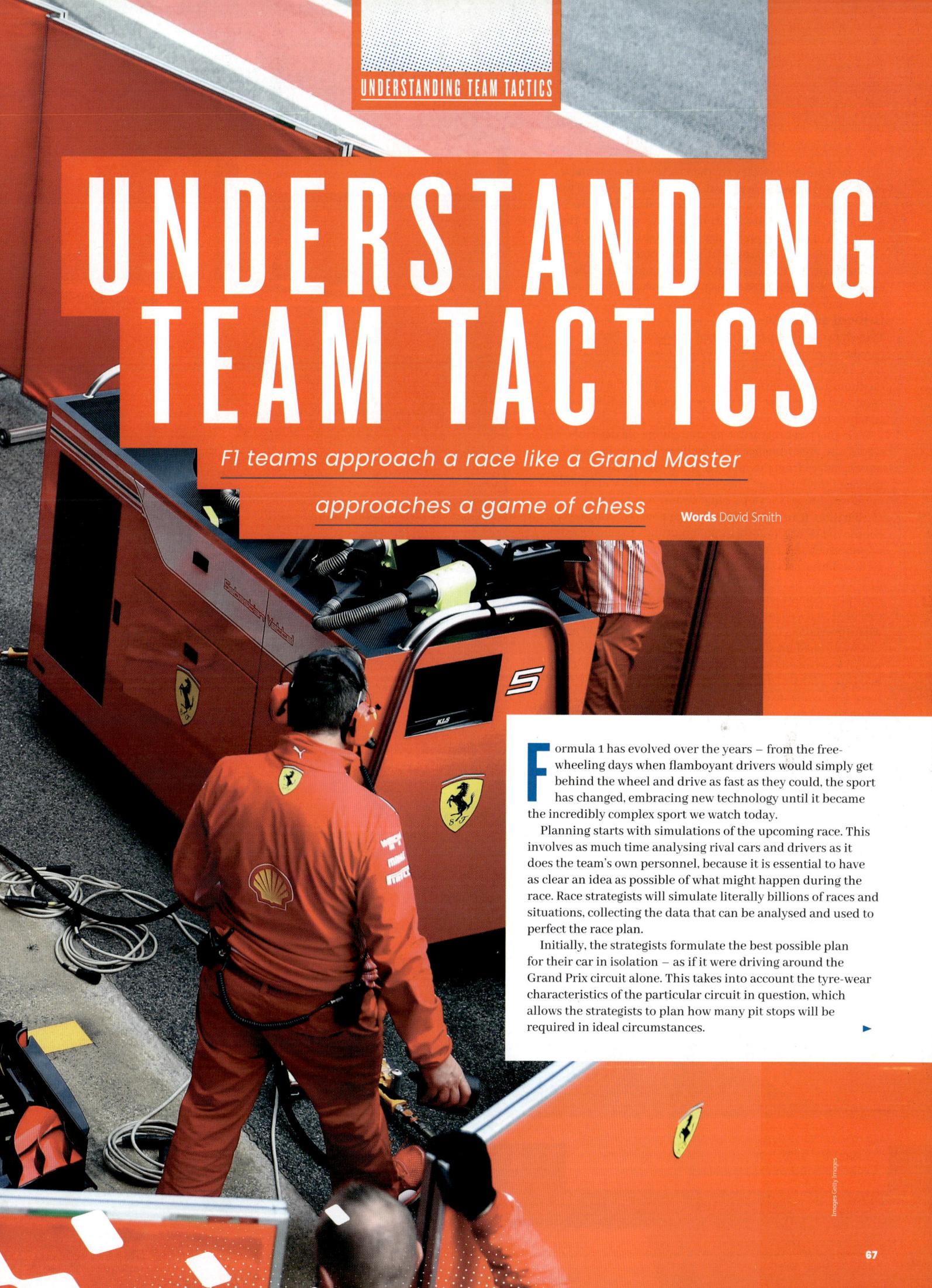

UNDERSTANDING TEAM TACTICS

UNDERSTANDING TEAM TACTICS

F1 teams approach a race like a Grand Master approaches a game of chess

Words David Smith

Formula 1 has evolved over the years – from the free-wheeling days when flamboyant drivers would simply get behind the wheel and drive as fast as they could, the sport has changed, embracing new technology until it became the incredibly complex sport we watch today.

Planning starts with simulations of the upcoming race. This involves as much time analysing rival cars and drivers as it does the team's own personnel, because it is essential to have as clear an idea as possible of what might happen during the race. Race strategists will simulate literally billions of races and situations, collecting the data that can be analysed and used to perfect the race plan.

Initially, the strategists formulate the best possible plan for their car in isolation – as if it were driving around the Grand Prix circuit alone. This takes into account the tyre-wear characteristics of the particular circuit in question, which allows the strategists to plan how many pit stops will be required in ideal circumstances. ▶

UNDERSTANDING TEAM TACTICS

The actions of other cars are then factored in, creating a more complex (but more realistic) model from which to work. As each element is added – tyre choice and pit strategies of opponents, how aggressive particular drivers are, what the weather is likely to be on the day – the possibilities expand exponentially. It is impossible to predict exactly how a race will turn out, but if enough data is collected it should be possible for a team to react instantly to a change in situation.

Critical elements

Tyre choice is obviously of crucial importance. Teams cannot simply pick the best tyre for the track and stick to it, they have to choose at least two compounds from the soft/medium/hard options, and the order in which the tyres are employed will impact on a car's performance at different times in the race.

Changing tyres requires a pit stop (in the old days this would also offer a chance for refuelling, but that has now been removed from the sport for safety reasons) and the timing of this is crucial. Although the race plan will include anticipated times for stops, other factors will play into the decision. If an opponent is slowing down, a team may choose to pit early (known as undercutting), to gain an extra advantage on new tyres. If a car is still running well on worn tyres, a pit stop may be delayed until after an opponent has pitted (known as overcutting). In this way, pit stops become tactical weapons that can gain a place in the race order if well executed, and this tactic is especially important on tracks where overtaking in open racing is difficult, such as Monaco.

A well-timed pit stop can also get a car out of a DRS train, where a stream of cars become locked together, unable to make use of their Drag Reduction System because the car in front is also able to engage it. A crafty pit stop can also be an option when a safety car is on the track – with everyone moving more slowly, the amount of time lost on the stop can be considerably reduced.

The choice of tyres and timing of pit stops can make or break a race strategy.

In mission control at the McLaren Technical Centre in Woking, the team monitor and analyse real-time data being transmitted from each race.

UNDERSTANDING TEAM TACTICS

The Red Bull team's pitwall command post during the São Paulo Grand Prix in 2023.

IN-RACE MONITORING

On the day of the race, data-gathering is even more critical than in the planning stage. Real-time data (known as telemetry) monitors such things as tyre temperature, engine performance and fuel consumption.

The vast amount of data is analysed and a team can make minute adjustments to squeeze an extra bit of performance out of the car – the fuel mix or suspension settings might be adjusted, for example. Teams also need to react quickly to unexpected developments, such as a crash, damage to their or an opponent's car, or a change in weather conditions. After a race, the telemetry remains valuable and can be used when planning for the same circuit next year.

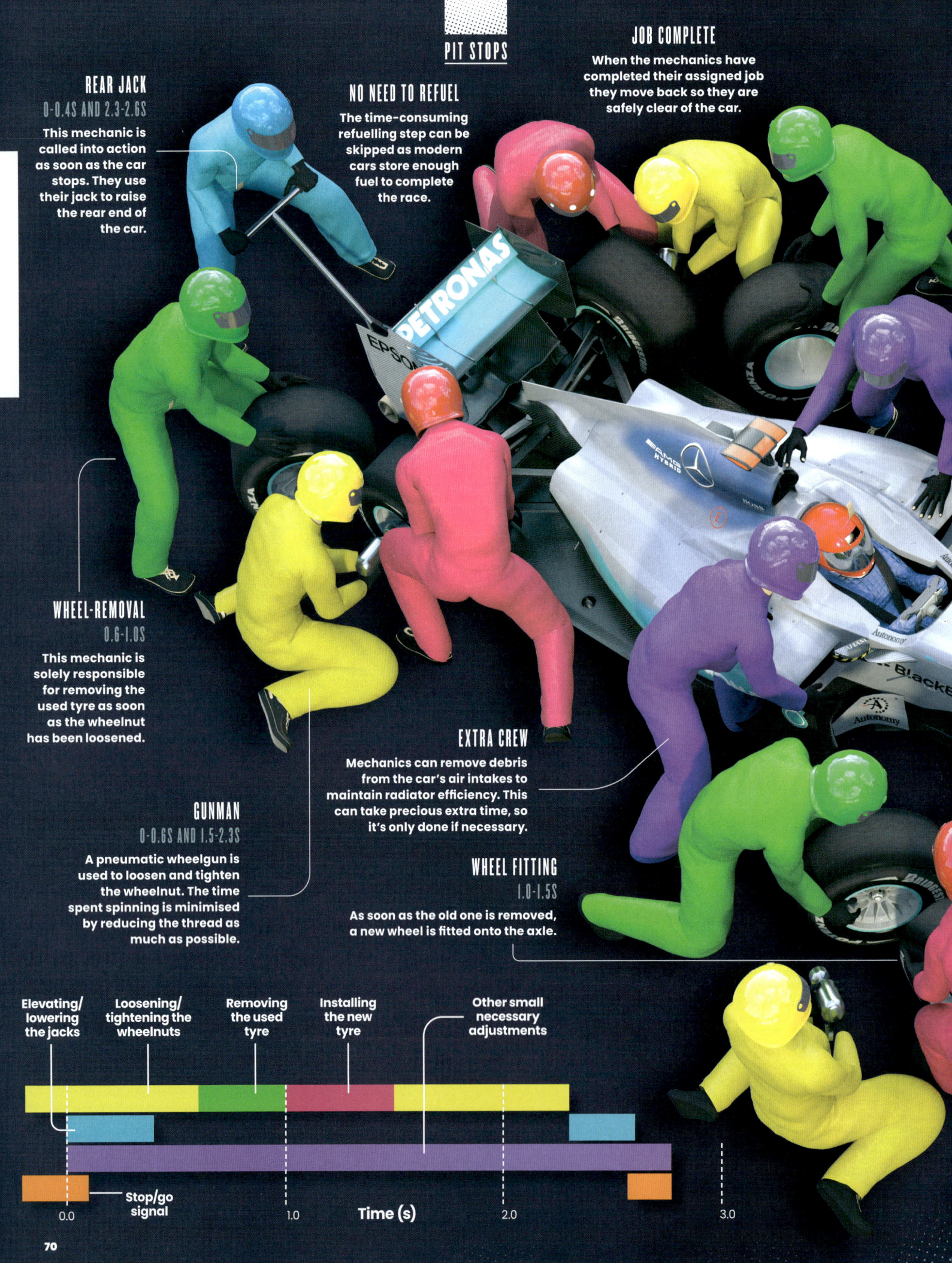

PIT STOPS

REAR JACK
0-0.4S AND 2.3-2.6S
This mechanic is called into action as soon as the car stops. They use their jack to raise the rear end of the car.

NO NEED TO REFUEL
The time-consuming refuelling step can be skipped as modern cars store enough fuel to complete the race.

JOB COMPLETE
When the mechanics have completed their assigned job they move back so they are safely clear of the car.

WHEEL-REMOVAL
0.6-1.0S
This mechanic is solely responsible for removing the used tyre as soon as the wheelnut has been loosened.

GUNMAN
0-0.6S AND 1.5-2.3S
A pneumatic wheelgun is used to loosen and tighten the wheelnut. The time spent spinning is minimised by reducing the thread as much as possible.

EXTRA CREW
Mechanics can remove debris from the car's air intakes to maintain radiator efficiency. This can take precious extra time, so it's only done if necessary.

WHEEL FITTING
1.0-1.5S
As soon as the old one is removed, a new wheel is fitted onto the axle.

Elevating/lowering the jacks | Loosening/tightening the wheelnuts | Removing the used tyre | Installing the new tyre | Other small necessary adjustments

Stop/go signal

Time (s)
0.0 1.0 2.0 3.0

Pit stops
How highly-trained teams perform engineering miracles at every race

In Formula 1, every second counts. The incredibly powerful cars are built for speed, but they need careful maintenance to complete a race. Fortunately, the driver's team of mechanics are ready and waiting in the pit lane to restore the car to an optimal condition in lightning-fast time. Before the car even pulls to a stop, the pit crews get to work on changing tyres, clearing debris and adjusting or exchanging parts of the vehicle.

By following a precise, rehearsed routine, teams complete their work in less than three seconds on average. And considering race winners have been decided by differences of under a fifth of a second, the best pit crew can be the difference a champion needs.

FIREFIGHTER
A crew with firefighting equipment are always ready in case of an emergency.

LOLLIPOP MAN
0-0.1S AND 2.6-2.8S

Named after the long 'stop/go' sign used to signal the driver, these days they give cues via a traffic light. Their role is to make sure it is safe for the driver to leave the pit lane.

EXPLOITING PIT STOP EFFICIENCY

Through watching the crews, the world has witnessed the benefits of detailed methodical planning and action. Away from the track, the healthcare and pharmaceutical industries hope to achieve the same levels of excellence by consulting with F1 teams. McLaren has helped drug manufacturer GlaxoSmithKline to switch production of toothpaste flavours in less than half of the original time, and the Williams team have advised doctors on improving their practice of resuscitating newborn babies. The University Hospital of Wales reorganised their equipment and created a floorplan with staff members assigned to specific places, and saw significant improvements as a result.

FRONT JACK
0-0.4S AND 2.3-2.6S

The jack is placed under the nose of the car to raise it off the ground.

ADJUSTMENT CREW
Team members are on hand to alter the angle of the wings, in order to increase or decrease downward force.

BELGIUM

SPA OFTEN TOPS DRIVERS' POLLS FOR THEIR FAVOURITE CIRCUIT OF ALL

Long straights and fast corners on a track set among the forests and rolling hills of the beautiful Ardennes region of Belgium make Spa one of F1's most loved circuits. Variable weather – from one part of the track to another, let alone one day to the next (created by those same spectacular Ardennes hills) – means grip can change in an instant. Eau Rouge, one of the most acclaimed series of corners found anywhere, leads in exhilarating fashion to the hill up through Raidillon. Lewis Hamilton has spoken of his enjoyment of the flat-out high g-force left-hander at Pouhon "which is swooping and downhill, so you arrive at incredible speeds".

THE LONGEST CIRCUIT ON THE CURRENT F1 ROSTER, SPA WAS ORIGINALLY TWICE AS LONG, AN INCREDIBLE 14.9KM (9.25MI).

PART OF THE MAIDEN F1 CHAMPIONSHIP IN 1950, THE FIRST RACE AT SPA WAS WON BY JUAN MANUEL FANGIO WHO LED AN ALFA ROMEO 1-2 AHEAD OF LUIGI FAGIOLI.

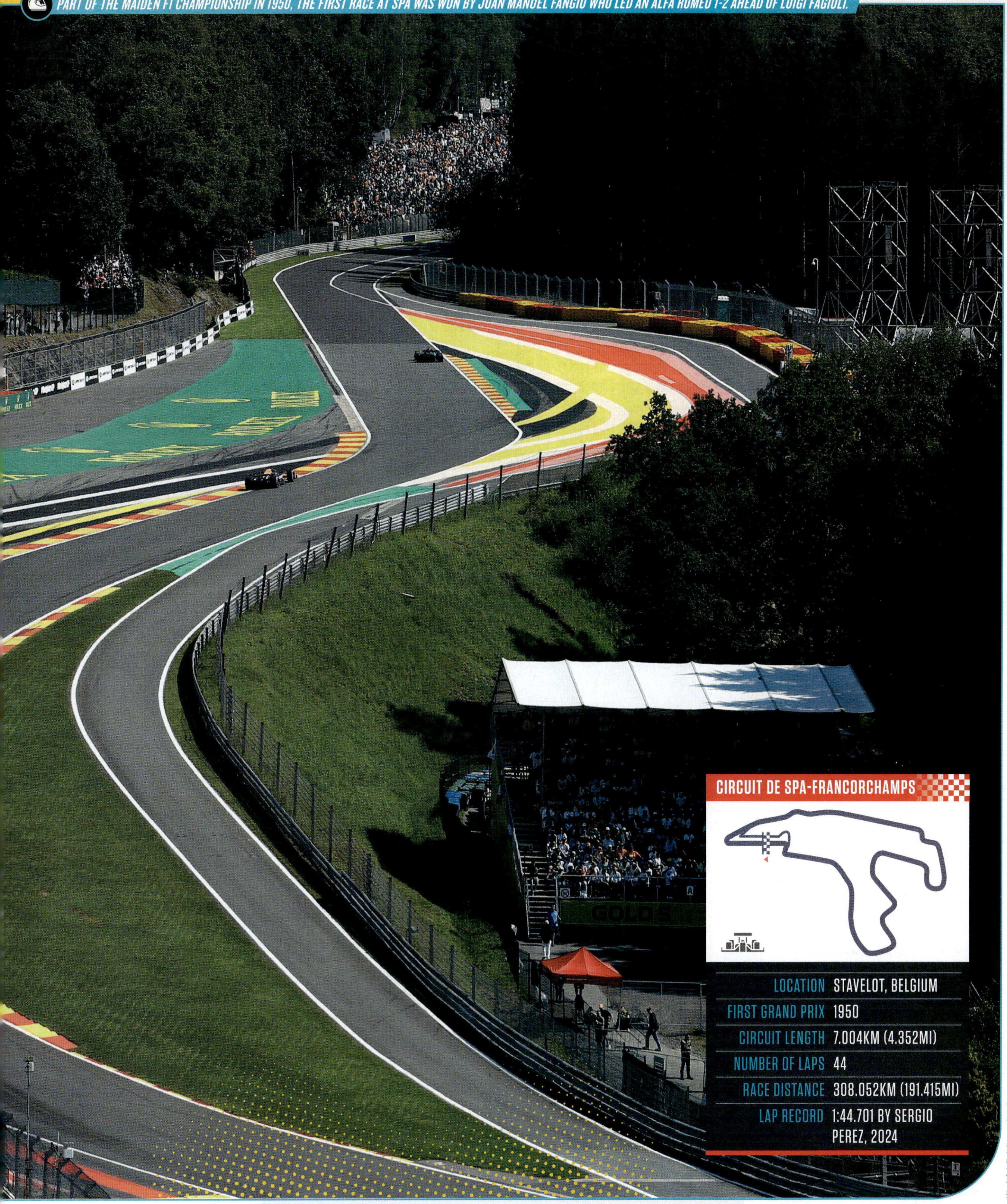

CIRCUIT DE SPA-FRANCORCHAMPS

LOCATION	STAVELOT, BELGIUM
FIRST GRAND PRIX	1950
CIRCUIT LENGTH	7.004KM (4.352MI)
NUMBER OF LAPS	44
RACE DISTANCE	308.052KM (191.415MI)
LAP RECORD	1:44.701 BY SERGIO PEREZ, 2024

Words Rob Clark, Images Getty Images

HUNGARY

THE FAMOUS HUNGARORING WILL BE HOSTING AN F1 RACE UNTIL AT LEAST 2032

It is a testament to how loved the Hungaroring is that it seems to have been part of the F1 calendar a lot longer than almost 40 years, but the purpose-built facility only opened in 1985. Its first race took place the following season and was won by Nelson Piquet. The circuit's lack of straights and numerous corners have seen it likened to a karting track, and certainly it requires serious levels of downforce. Chassis prep and setup are more important than outright speed, with finding a good rhythm often being the key to consistently fast lap times – which might explain why Lewis Hamilton has won the race a record eight times.

HUNGARORING

LOCATION	BUDAPEST, HUNGARY
FIRST GRAND PRIX	1986
CIRCUIT LENGTH	4.381KM (2.722MI)
NUMBER OF LAPS	70
RACE DISTANCE	306.63KM (190.53MI)
LAP RECORD	1:16.627 BY LEWIS HAMILTON, 2020

THE 1986 HUNGARIAN GRAND PRIX WAS A COUP FOR BERNIE ECCLESTONE, BEING THE FIRST F1 RACE TO TAKE PLACE BEHIND THE IRON CURTAIN.

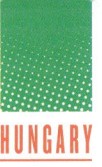

INCREDIBLY, DAMON HILL, FERNANDO ALONSO, JENSEN BUTTON, HEIKKI KOVALAINEN, ESTEBAN OCON AND OSCAR PIASTRI ALL RECORDED THEIR MAIDEN GP WINS AT THE HUNGARORING.

Words Rob Clark; Images Getty Images

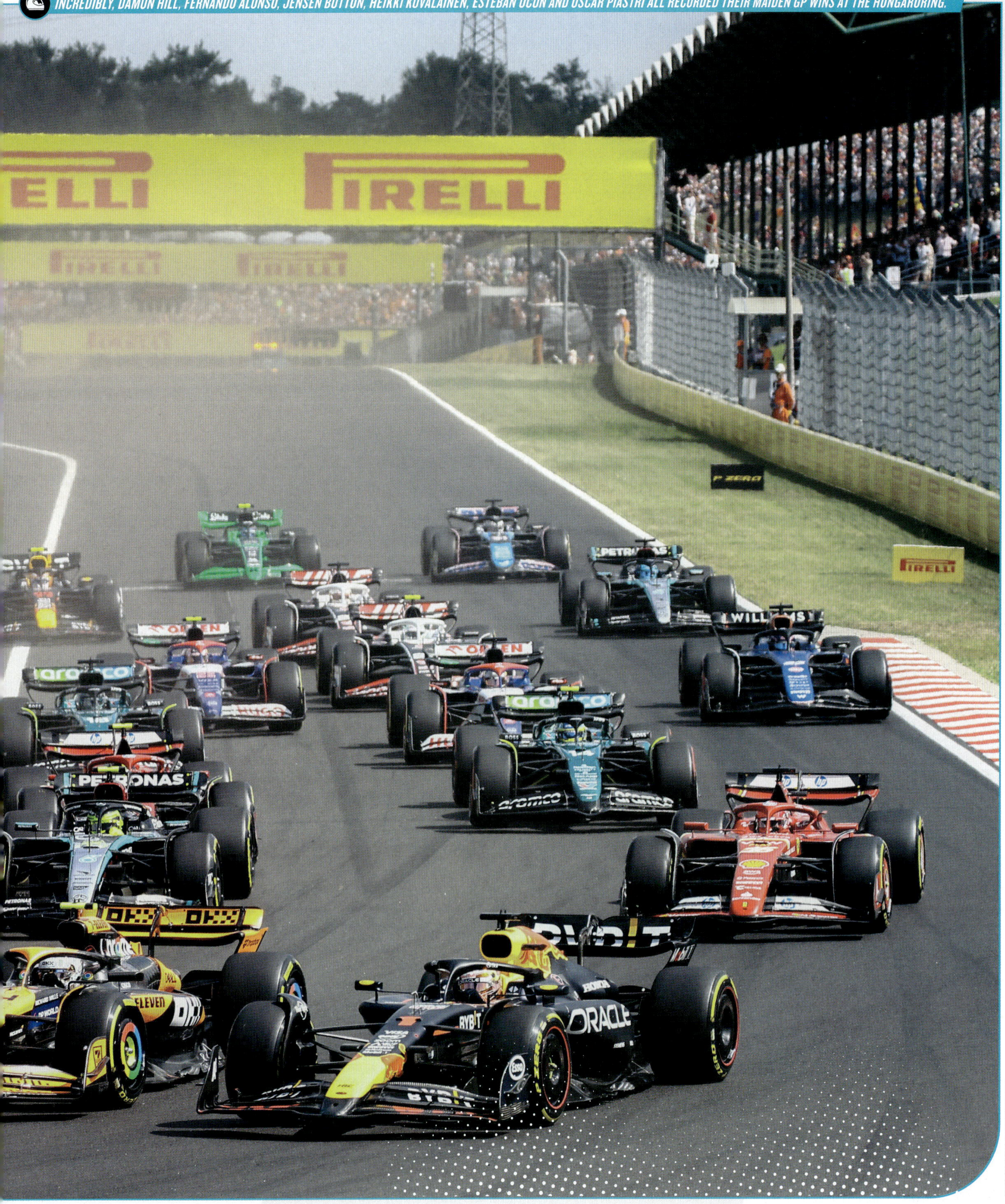

NETHERLANDS

ZANDVOORT'S F1 HISTORY IS PATCHY, BUT IT ALWAYS PROVIDES EXCITING RACING

Like Silverstone, Zandvoort was built in 1948 as part of the post-war motorsport boom across Europe, with the original design a 4.2km (2.6mi) track that combined the use of some public roads with a permanent track that wound its way through the sand dunes of the pretty Dutch resort town. When the first F1 race as part of the World Championship was held, in 1952, Alberto Ascari led home a Ferrari 1-2-3. In 1985, Zandvoort dropped off the F1 calendar, but it returned in 2021 and retains its undulating, rollercoaster-like feel amid the dunes, which makes it a quick, challenging track. The atmosphere during Max Verstappen's recent domination has been incredible.

THE SO-CALLED TARZAN CORNER FEATURES 18 DEGREES OF BANKING AND PROVIDES A DRAMATIC BUT SCARY MOMENT FOR THE DRIVERS.

NETHERLANDS

VERSTAPPEN WON THE FIRST THREE RACES AT THE NEW ZANDVOORT, HIS RUN ONLY ENDED BY LANDO NORRIS IN 2024. 2026 WILL BE THE LAST RACE ON THE CIRCUIT.

CIRCUIT ZANDVOORT

LOCATION	ZANDVOORT, THE NETHERLANDS
FIRST GRAND PRIX	1952
CIRCUIT LENGTH	4.259KM (2.646MI)
NUMBER OF LAPS	72
RACE DISTANCE	306.587KM (190.504MI)
LAP RECORD	1:11.097 BY LEWIS HAMILTON, 2021

Rivalries

Formula 1 is built on the rivalries between drivers, and while most are friendly, others occasionally get out of hand...

Words Rob Clark

Stirling Moss v Juan Manuel Fangio
1951-1958

Widely recognised as the greatest driver never to win the World Championship, Moss nevertheless always felt that Fangio was the better driver. On one occasion he declared: "Winning [the World Championship] ten times wouldn't make me a better driver, because I'm not. Fangio was better than I was, and that's that. In the sportscars I could beat him... but in a Formula 1 car he simply drove the thing round the corner faster than anyone else." For his part, Fangio acknowledged Moss to be his most serious rival, but their rivalry was underpinned by a genuine friendship which endured throughout their careers.

RIVALRIES

Jim Clark v Graham Hill
1960–1968

As with Fangio and Moss before them, the rivalry between Clark and Hill was born out of respect for each other's talent and driving ability. As people, they were completely different – Clark was from an affluent farming family and had been driving all his life, whereas Hill came from a poor background and didn't start racing until he was 24. Both won the world title twice, and both also won the Indy 500 (Clark in 1965, Hill a year later). Yet even when they were both driving for Lotus there was never any conflict between them, they raced fairly and applauded each other's victories.

Niki Lauda v James Hunt
1973–1979

Austrian driver Lauda was precise, analytical, focused; Hunt was dynamic, charismatic and entertaining. And yet they were such good friends that they even stayed with each other on occasion. Their friendship dated back to their Formula 3 days when they travelled around Europe together, living on a shoestring but enjoying themselves, in London and elsewhere. Even in 1976 when Lauda suffered his horrendous crash and Hunt snatched the title by a single point, there remained mutual respect. Of Lauda's comeback from his burns, Hunt said simply: "I think Niki Lauda is the bravest guy I have ever met."

RIVALRIES

Ayrton Senna v Alain Prost
1984–1993

The disregard Prost and Senna had for each other was probably grounded in their being such totally different personalities, on and off the track. Prost was nicknamed 'the Professor' in recognition of his studied, intellectual approach to racing. Senna, by contrast, was a whirlwind who blew into Formula 1 and drove flat out all the time. For arguably the first time in F1, the antagonism became physical in 1988 with Senna threatening to drive Prost into the pitwall if he tried to overtake. In 1989, Prost deliberately turned into Senna's inside line, and in 1990 Senna intentionally crashed into Prost to preserve his lead in the championship.

Nigel Mansell v Nelson Piquet
1980–1991

Piquet and Mansell were, it's safe to say, never good friends. In 1986 and 1987 they were Williams teammates, but with both in contention for the title it was always going to be difficult keeping them happy all the time. Mansell was the number two driver but focused all his physical strength and willingness to take risks on the task at hand. Although Piquet won three world titles to Mansell's one, the Briton won more races (31 to 23), and also won the American CART title. Mansell said that their racing, though hard, stayed fair. And Piquet concurred: "We never crashed into each other. In no championship did we do that."

RIVALRIES

Michael Schumacher v Damon Hill
1992–1999

The German driver is one of the sport's all-time greats, but he underestimated Hill and didn't initially give the British driver the credit he deserved. As a result he chose to take more direct action in defending his position, and frequently found himself penalised because of it. In 1994, Schumacher made a rash manoeuvre which took Hill out; most observers felt that Schumacher was in the wrong, but as he had just sealed the World Championship, no action was taken against him. In 1995, Schumacher dominated and in 1996 Hill finally got the title he deserved, but throughout those three seasons no quarter was given.

Fernando Alonso v Kimi Räikkönen
2001–2009, 2012–2018, 2021

Alonso, the champion in 2005 and 2006, and Räikkönen, champion in 2007, dominated F1 for a three-year period. They made their F1 debuts in the same race: the 2001 Australian Grand Prix. Alonso finished 12th in his Minardi, Räikkönen sixth in the Sauber-Petronas. Little did we suspect that 13 years later they would share a season with Ferrari in 2014, when Alonso had much the better of the dual. The two men shared similar skillsets in their cool, concentrated approach to racing – Räikkönen appeared relaxed and laidback, but was a determined racer. And both men were fast, very fast.

RIVALRIES

Sebastian Vettel v Lewis Hamilton
2008–2022

Having won his first World Championship with McLaren Mercedes in 2008, Hamilton had a ringside seat for Vettel's four consecutive titles from 2010 to 2013 in what was then Red Bull Renault. Hamilton later made up for those years stranded in an uncompetitive car, equalling Schumacher's seven world titles, and setting records for most wins, most poles, most podiums and many fastest laps. Vettel and Hamilton were involved in genuine contests in 2017 and, especially, 2018 when both were looking for a fifth title. Hamilton has said that his battles with Vettel were among his favourites and that the respect between them "is huge".

RIVALRIES

Lewis Hamilton v Max Verstappen
2015-Present

Hamilton sets great store by what he considers "clean racing". While whip-sharp overtaking moves have always been a part of his armoury, Hamilton has a firm grasp of the bigger picture and wider responsibilities and has, on occasion, backed out of potential clashes in order to live to fight another day. That is anathema to the aggressive Dutchman who goes for every opportunity, a style perfectly summed up by events in Abu Dhabi in 2021 (pictured) – it wasn't Verstappen's fault that the rules were wrongly applied, but he took full advantage to snatch a win that he didn't fully deserve.

George Russell v Max Verstappen
2019-Present

While it was Lando Norris who applied pressure to Verstappen's ultimately successful pursuit of a fourth consecutive Drivers' Championship, it was another British driver who caused sparks to fly off the track. Verstappen and Russell had had words in 2022, but before the 2024 Abu Dhabi Grand Prix it turned into a full-blown row. Russell accused Verstappen of being a bully and said that "he cannot deal with adversity", while Verstappen felt Russell was out of order for pushing for a penalty against him in qualifying. If Russell has a competitive car in 2025, we could see more clashes to come.

ITALY

THE HISTORIC MONZA CIRCUIT OFFERS FAST RACING IN A SPECTACULAR SETTING

The acclaimed Monza circuit, home of the Italian Grand Prix ever since 1950, is quick. Very quick. Cars are at full throttle for a large proportion of the race and have to negotiate a series of chicanes which they approach at ultra-high speeds, requiring a lot of work on the brakes. At the Variante de Rettifilo, for example, they have to slow from around 350kph to just 70kph (217mph to 43mph) – a perfect opportunity for overtaking if a driver gets it wrong. The circuit's emphasis on straightline speed and engine reliability often leads to a high attrition rate and the track has sadly also claimed the lives of top drivers Alberto Ascari (1955), Wolfgang von Trips (1961), Jochen Rindt (1970) and Ronnie Peterson (1978).

DURING QUALIFICATION FOR THE 2020 ITALIAN GRAND PRIX AT MONZA, LEWIS HAMILTON BROKE THE WORLD RECORD FOR THE HIGHEST AVERAGE LAP SPEED OVER A

MONZA, WHICH SITS JUST OUTSIDE MILAN, IS LOCATED IN A LARGE PUBLIC PARK AND IS LARGELY SET AMONGST WOODLAND, MAKING FOR A PICTURESQUE BACKDROP.

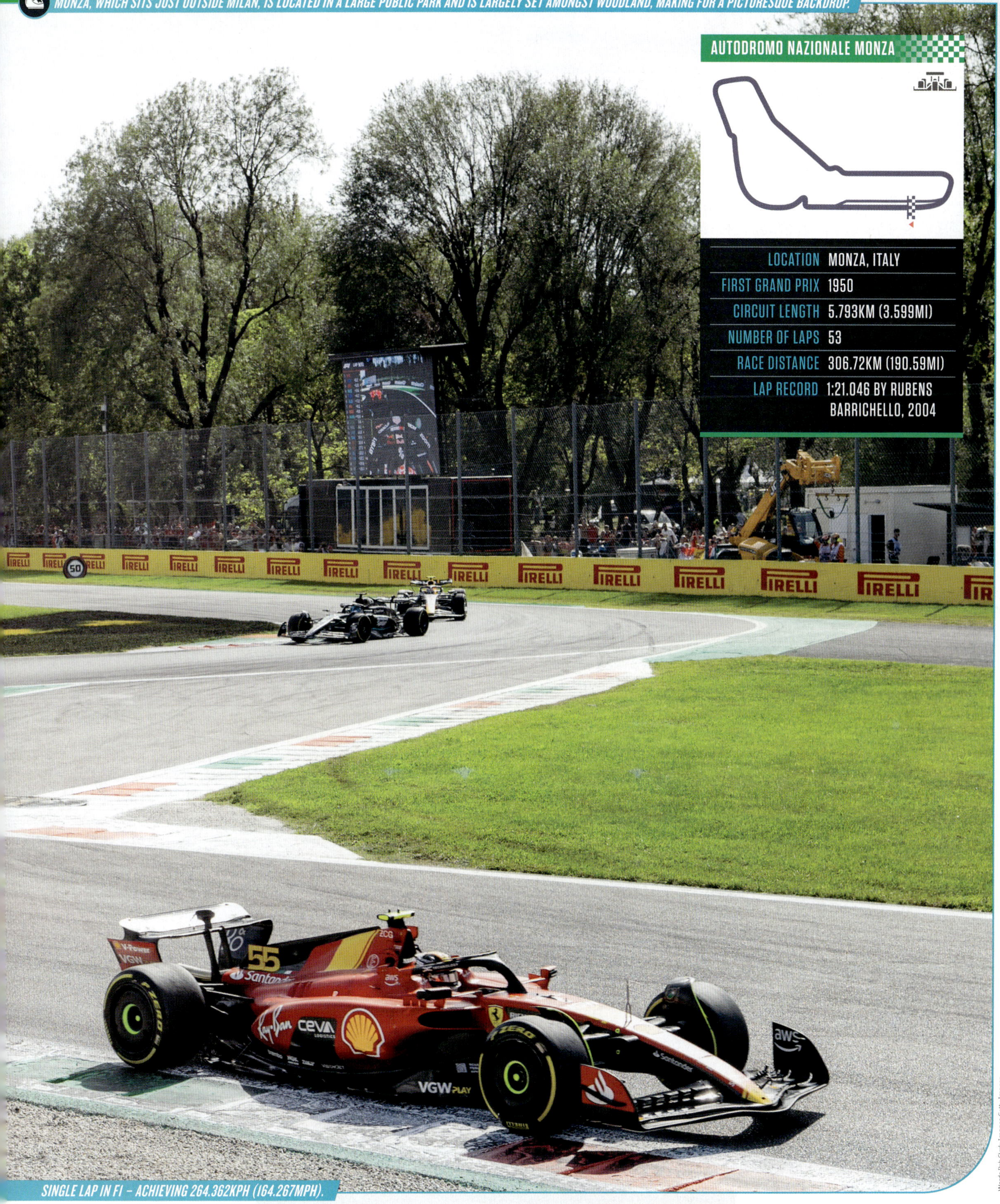

AUTODROMO NAZIONALE MONZA

LOCATION	MONZA, ITALY
FIRST GRAND PRIX	1950
CIRCUIT LENGTH	5.793KM (3.599MI)
NUMBER OF LAPS	53
RACE DISTANCE	306.72KM (190.59MI)
LAP RECORD	1:21.046 BY RUBENS BARRICHELLO, 2004

SINGLE LAP IN F1 – ACHIEVING 264.362KPH (164.267MPH).

Words Rob Clark; Images Getty Images

AZERBAIJAN

AZERBAIJAN HAS BEEN A WELCOME ADDITION TO THE GRAND PRIX CALENDAR

The first Grand Prix to take place on the Baku street circuit was the 2016 European Grand Prix. The inaugural Azerbaijan Grand Prix followed a year later and witnessed a surprise winner in Australian Daniel Ricciardo. The circuit is an intriguing mixture of fast open straights and tight turns – the end of the main straight affords an ideal viewing point as the cars are able to run three abreast into the approach to Turn 1, while the hard braking provides the opportunity to slipstream and overtake. From there the circuit moves away from the shoreline and into the old part of the medieval city with its narrow streets, leading to a different type of challenge for drivers and cars.

IN THE SEVEN RUNNINGS OF THE AZERBAIJAN GRAND PRIX TO DATE (IT WAS CANCELLED IN 2020), SERGIO PÉREZ IS THE ONLY DRIVER TO HAVE WON TWICE.

AZERBAIJAN

THE 2023 RACE BECAME THE FIRST GRAND PRIX TO IMPLEMENT THE NEW 'SPRINT SHOOTOUT' FORMAT DURING QUALIFYING.

BAKU CITY CIRCUIT

LOCATION	BAKU, AZERBAIJAN
FIRST GRAND PRIX	2016
CIRCUIT LENGTH	6.003KM (3.730MI)
NUMBER OF LAPS	51
RACE DISTANCE	306.049KM (190.170MI)
LAP RECORD	1:43.009 BY CHARLES LECLERC, 2019

SINGAPORE

FIRST RUN IN 2008, THE SINGAPORE GRAND PRIX WAS AN INSTANT HIT

The appeal of the Singapore Grand Prix can be summed up by the name of the circuit on which it is held: it is both a stunning harbourside setting in downtown Singapore and a winding street track featuring 19 turns (reduced from 23 in 2023). This makes for a physically demanding circuit as the humidity of early autumn combined with an excessively bumpy track are tough conditions for the drivers. Pre-Covid the race was dominated by Sebastian Vettel (five wins) and Lewis Hamilton (four wins), but since that two-year hiatus there have been three different winners in Sergio Pérez, Carlos Sainz and Lando Norris.

THE FIRST EDITION OF THE SINGAPORE GRAND PRIX WAS ALSO THE FIRST NIGHT-TIME RACE IN F1 HISTORY.

SINGAPORE

EVERY YEAR FROM 2008-2023 SAW AT LEAST ONE APPEARANCE OF THE SAFETY CAR AT SINGAPORE; 2024'S RACE WAS THE FIRST THAT DID NOT.

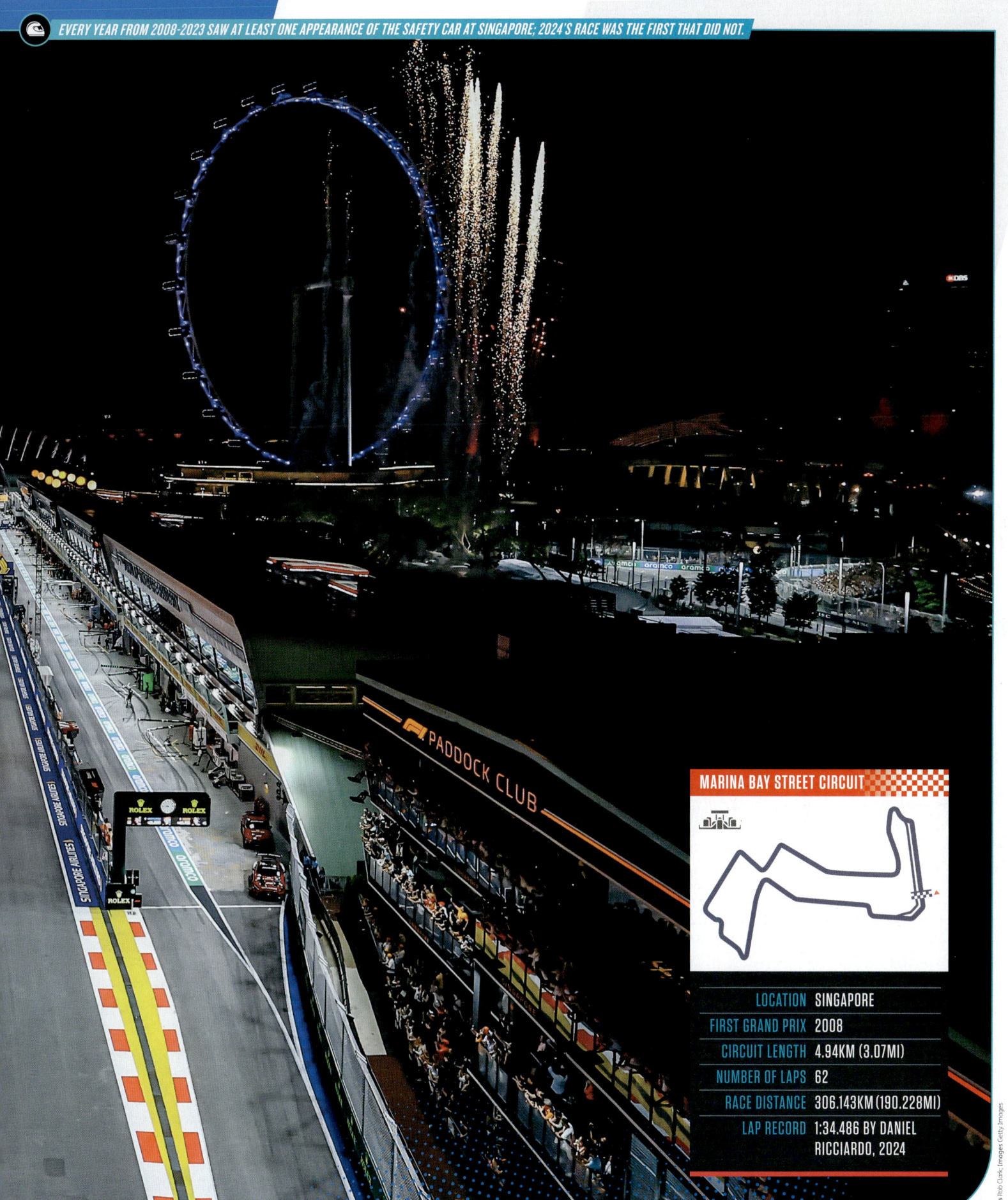

MARINA BAY STREET CIRCUIT

LOCATION	SINGAPORE
FIRST GRAND PRIX	2008
CIRCUIT LENGTH	4.94KM (3.07MI)
NUMBER OF LAPS	62
RACE DISTANCE	306.143KM (190.228MI)
LAP RECORD	1:34.486 BY DANIEL RICCIARDO, 2024

2024 IN REVIEW

Last year's championship looked set to be a repeat of 2023, but McLaren thought otherwise. Here's how the 2024 season unfolded...

Words Rob Clark

2024 IN REVIEW

At the start of the 2024 F1 season, it seemed likely we'd be in for another year of total dominance by Max Verstappen and the Red Bull team. Verstappen won four of the first five races, seven of the first ten, and by the halfway point he was way out in front of the chasing pack. The other five had been won by Carlos Sainz and Charles Leclerc in their Ferraris, Lando Norris in his McLaren-Mercedes and George Russell and Lewis Hamilton in their Mercedes, so it wasn't even as if there was a clear direct rival to Verstappen.

It seemed likely that the young Dutchman would go on to exhibit the same level of control as 2022, when he won 15 out of 22 races and took the World Drivers' title by 146 points, and 2023 when he won an unbelievable 19 out of 22 races to take the title by a ridiculous margin of 290 points.

In the event, though, Verstappen didn't win again between the tenth race – the Spanish Grand Prix in Barcelona – and the 21st, the Brazilian Grand Prix in São Paulo. Ultimately,

The drivers pose together for a portrait at the start of the 2024 season in Bahrain.

Verstappen had already done enough to claim his fourth consecutive Drivers' Championship, but his drop-off in form in the second half of the season cost Red Bull their third consecutive Constructors' Championship.

Changes

For the first time in F1 history, all driver and team combinations which finished the 2023 season started in 2024.

In terms of the calendar, stability was the name of the game there too. The Chinese Grand Prix returned to the calendar after a four-year absence (caused by the Covid-19 pandemic), while the Emilia-Romagna Grand Prix, cancelled at short notice in 2023 on account of severe flooding in the region, was also restored.

There were also only minor changes to the F1 regulations, with the sport seemingly taking a 'steady as she goes' approach prior to the major technical changes planned for the 2026 season. The sprint events were further separated from the main race by holding them before the qualifying session on a Saturday, while DRS usage was now permitted one lap after the start, a safety car restart or a red flag restart rather than two, something which had been trialled in 2023. The power unit allocation was increased from three to four per season per driver, and this change will remain in place for the 2025 season.

Highlights and headlights

But if the start of the season largely saw the status quo maintained, the Miami Grand Prix, the sixth race of the season, proved to be a game-changer in terms of the speed of the leading cars. It was here that McLaren introduced a technical upgrade which included a better balance between suspension and aerodynamics via a new front wing. For two years, Red Bull had been leading the pack in this aspect, but now McLaren had caught up – and even moved ahead.

McLaren's win ended over 20 years of Constructors' Championship dominance by Red Bull and Mercedes.

Lando Norris celebrates his first F1 race victory in Miami with the McLaren team.

McLaren's technical upgrades turned out to be a game-changer.

2024 IN REVIEW

DHL FASTEST LAP AWARD 2024
Awarded for the total number of fastest laps in the season

- MAX VERSTAPPEN — RED BULL — 3 — =2
- LANDO NORRIS — MCLAREN — 6 — 1
- CHARLES LECLERC — FERRARI — 3 — =2

2024 CONSTRUCTORS STANDINGS

PLACE	TEAM	POINTS
1	MCLAREN	666
2	FERRARI	652
3	RED BULL	589
4	MERCEDES	468
5	ASTON MARTIN	94
6	ALPINE	65
7	HAAS	58
8	RB	46
9	WILLIAMS	17
10	KICK SAUBER	4

2024 IN REVIEW

Max Verstappen managed to secure the 2024 championship with his victory at the Las Vegas Grand Prix.

Sergio Pérez and Red Bull parted ways after he had a disappointing end to the 2024 season

2024 DRIVERS STANDINGS

PLACE	DRIVER	TEAM	POINTS
1	MAX VERSTAPPEN	RED BULL	437
2	LANDO NORRIS	MCLAREN	374
3	CHARLES LECLERC	FERRARI	356
4	OSCAR PIASTRI	MCLAREN	292
5	CARLOS SAINZ	FERRARI	290
6	GEORGE RUSSELL	MERCEDES	245
7	LEWIS HAMILTON	MERCEDES	223
8	SERGIO PÉREZ	RED BULL	152
9	FERNANDO ALONSO	ASTON MARTIN	70
10	PIERRE GASLY	ALPINE	42
11	NICO HÜLKENBERG	HAAS	41
12	YUKI TSUNODA	RB	30
13	LANCE STROLL	ASTON MARTIN	24
14	ESTEBAN OCON	ALPINE	23
15	KEVIN MAGNUSSEN	HAAS	16
16	ALEXANDER ALBON	WILLIAMS	12
17	DANIEL RICCIARDO†	RB	12
18	OLIVER BEARMAN*	HAAS	7
19	FRANCO COLAPINTO‡	WILLIAMS	5
20	ZHOU GUANYU	KICK SAUBER	4
21	LIAM LAWSON†	RB	4
22	VALTTERI BOTTAS	KICK SAUBER	0
23	LOGAN SARGEANT‡	WILLIAMS	0
24	JACK DOOHAN*	ALPINE	0

*Reserve drivers
†Lawson replaced Ricciardo mid-season
‡Colapinto replaced Sargeant mid-season

Charles Leclerc and the Ferrari team celebrating the win in Monaco.

Oscar Piastri's consistent performance all year helped McLaren clinch the Constructors' title.

As a result, Norris claimed his maiden Grand Prix victory at Miami, and though in the end he didn't have quite the experience to sustain a challenge to Verstappen's lead, he did win a further three races. Significantly, however, the McLaren car was, from this point on, often faster than the Red Bull. And interestingly, a Verstappen under pressure proved to be far from unflappable; although to give him his due, he secured the title with one of the all-time great wet-weather drives in Brazil.

If McLaren's improvement was the biggest news in the Constructors' title race, Ferrari's return to the top table was equally welcome. Sergio Pérez's lack of form (which has cost him his place for 2025) meant that Red Bull were no longer able to hold off their rivals and the Constructors' Championship came down to a battle between McLaren and Ferrari, which went to the final race of the season in Abu Dhabi. There, a masterly drive from Norris ensured the title went to McLaren, despite Sainz and Leclerc completing the podium. It was McLaren's first triumph of the century, their last title coming in 1998, and CEO Zak Brown paid a fulsome tribute to team principal Andrea Stella: "He leads by example, he pushes everyone to get the best out of them and he's done such a good job of leading this team."

> "HAMILTON'S MOVE TO FERRARI WAS NOT ONLY BREAKING UP THE MOST SUCCESSFUL DRIVER-CAR PARTNERSHIP IN F1 HISTORY, IT TOTALLY SHOOK UP THE DRIVER MARKET"

Driver highlights included Leclerc's historic victory at Monaco, the first for a Monaco native since 1931 and therefore the first ever in the 75-year history of the official World Championship. Leclerc was equally good at Monza, utilising a bold, one-stop strategy to the delight of the Tifosi.

And Oscar Piastri, in just his second season in F1, claimed a maiden Grand Prix win in Hungary. If that victory was under a slight cloud in that Piastri benefitted from team orders, his potential was underlined when he added another win in Azerbaijan. His consistency all year – Piastri only finished outside the top 10 once all season, and had no retirements – played a massive part in McLaren's Constructors' Championship title, and he undoubtedly has the talent to finish higher than the fourth place he managed in 2024.

Shocks and surprises

The most surprising news of 2024 came before the season even got underway, with the announcement that Lewis Hamilton would be moving to Ferrari for 2025. Not only was this breaking up the most successful driver-car partnership in F1 history, but it totally shook up the entire driver market and initially left Sainz without a drive for 2025. It was inevitable that Sainz would be in demand, however, and later in the season it was confirmed that he would be going to Williams, whose team principal James Vowles has long admitted to being an admirer.

Arguably the next biggest surprise move wasn't by a driver at all, but rather by designer Adrian Newey. After nearly 20 years with Red Bull, Newey announced he would be leaving for pastures new. Where those pastures would be wasn't revealed until later in the season, but it turned out to be Aston Martin. The offer of partnership and shares was what attracted Newey, but for us fans what it most signals is the intent on the part of Aston Martin and team owner Lawrence Stroll.

Were there issues at Red Bull? Sporting director Jonathan Wheatley left to join Sauber and advisor Helmut Marko also appeared on the verge of being eased out until Verstappen made it plain that if that happened, he would leave too.

Teenager Ollie Bearman made an impressive showing as a replacement for Sainz (who had appendicitis) by finishing seventh at the Saudi Arabian Grand Prix. It earned him a full-time seat with Haas for 2025, while Haas themselves shocked the paddock by proving they had more resilience than previously suspected after finishing in seventh place in the Constructors' Championship.

Penalties and controversies

The most notable driver penalty of 2024 was that meted out to Verstappen for his use of the f-word during a press conference in Singapore. The first victim of the FIA's attempt to clamp down on bad language in public, Verstappen was 'sentenced' to community service and undertook two days' work at a grassroots motorsport program in Rwanda, ahead of the FIA Awards ceremony in Kigali. Leclerc was fined €10,000 (~£8,000/$10,000) for the same offence in Mexico City, though half of the fine was suspended as long as he does not commit the same offence again in a 12-month period.

Kevin Magnussen made an unwanted piece of F1 history by becoming the first driver to suffer a one-race ban for exceeding 12 penalty points over a 12-month period. His final offence was when he was deemed responsible for a crash with Pierre Gasly at Turn 4 of the Italian Grand Prix. Magnussen admitted he couldn't quite see the problem: "We had a slight contact, no damage on either car, no consequences. We both missed the

Lewis Hamilton at a farewell event hosted by McLaren, ahead of his move to Ferrari.

At the end of the 2024 season, Carlos Sainz left Ferrari and signed a two-year deal with Williams.

2024 IN REVIEW

Former Ferrari reserve driver Oliver Bearman impressed in 2024, leading to a multi-year deal with Haas.

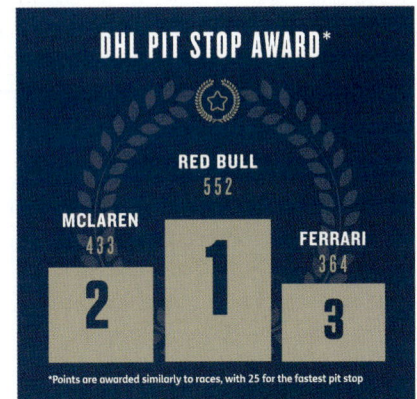

DHL PIT STOP AWARD*

- 1. RED BULL — 552
- 2. McLAREN — 433
- 3. FERRARI — 364

*Points are awarded similarly to races, with 25 for the fastest pit stop

FASTEST PIT STOP

- =1. MAX VERSTAPPEN, RED BULL, CHINA — 1.90s
- =1. OSCAR PIASTRI, McLAREN, MEXICO — 1.90s
- 2. MAX VERSTAPPEN, RED BULL, SPAIN — 1.92s

2024 IN REVIEW

Kevin Magnussen was penalised after a controversial clash with Pierre Gasly at Monza, leading to a rare one-race ban.

In Singapore, Max Verstappen fell foul of the FIA's crackdown on bad language.

MOST PODIUMS: DRIVERS

MAX VERSTAPPEN — 14 — 1

CHARLES LECLERC — 13 — =2

LANDO NORRIS — 13 — =2

2024 IN REVIEW

Charles Leclerc received a fine for bad language during a press conference in Mexico City.

corner, but, hey, we're racing." Despite this, Magnussen was forced to miss the next race.

As for controversies, they perhaps weren't as plentiful as they have been in some F1 seasons, although the rivalry between Verstappen and Norris got quite tasty as the latter proved himself an increasing threat. The Dutchman got more and more aggressive in his driving style, most notably in the USA and Mexico, and came in for some criticism that he was overstepping the mark.

The Dutch driver was also critical of some of the technical advances other teams made, and came perilously close to accusing McLaren of cheating, which the title-winning team denied. The FIA almost completely backed McLaren, finding no fault with its flexible front wings, nor its water injections used to cool tyres.

Looking ahead

The 2024 F1 season ended up being a much more exciting affair than it promised at the start, and over the first few races. Verstappen won his fourth consecutive World Drivers' Championship, an impressive feat. But there were signs other drivers may, possibly, be just as good as the Dutch star given competitive cars.

And even clearer signs that Red Bull were no longer the dominant force, as McLaren and Ferrari had caught up, and others were not far behind. Red Bull looked rattled. They started accusing other teams of playing fast and loose with the rules, accusations which did not stand up, and their leading driver occasionally lost his cool. More of the same for 2025 please.

MOST PODIUMS: TEAMS
- FERRARI 22 — 1
- MCLAREN 21 — 2
- RED BULL 18 — 3

Max Verstappen and Lando Norris had several close encounters on the track throughout the season.

UNITED STATES

THE SECOND OF THREE AMERICAN GRANDS PRIX, COTA IS A GREAT CIRCUIT FOR RACING

Designer Hermann Tilke, in conjunction with American architects HKS, built the Texan circuit, which opened in 2012. Despite being only 13 years old in 2025, Tilke has made the track look remarkably familiar through the simple expedient of copying sections of other older, more famous circuits. So Turns 3-6 resemble the high-speed corners of Silverstone and the S curves at Suzuka. Turns 12-15 meanwhile look like Hockenheim's famous stadium section, while Turn 1's fast and very wide uphill run allows lots of overtaking. COTA, as it's commonly known, is the first circuit in the USA to be purpose-built for F1, though it does now host other motorsports events as well, and has proved popular with the drivers.

THE CIRCUIT SITS ON AN 800-ACRE PLOT OF LAND TO THE EAST OF AUSTIN, TEXAS, AND IS THE SIXTH TRACK TO BE USED FOR THE F1 UNITED STATES GRAND PRIX.

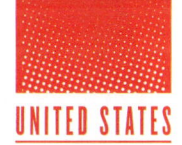

LEWIS HAMILTON HAS WON THE RACE ON FIVE OUT OF THE 12 OCCASIONS IT HAS BEEN HELD AT COTA, INCLUDING FOUR CONSECUTIVE TIMES BETWEEN 2014 AND 2017.

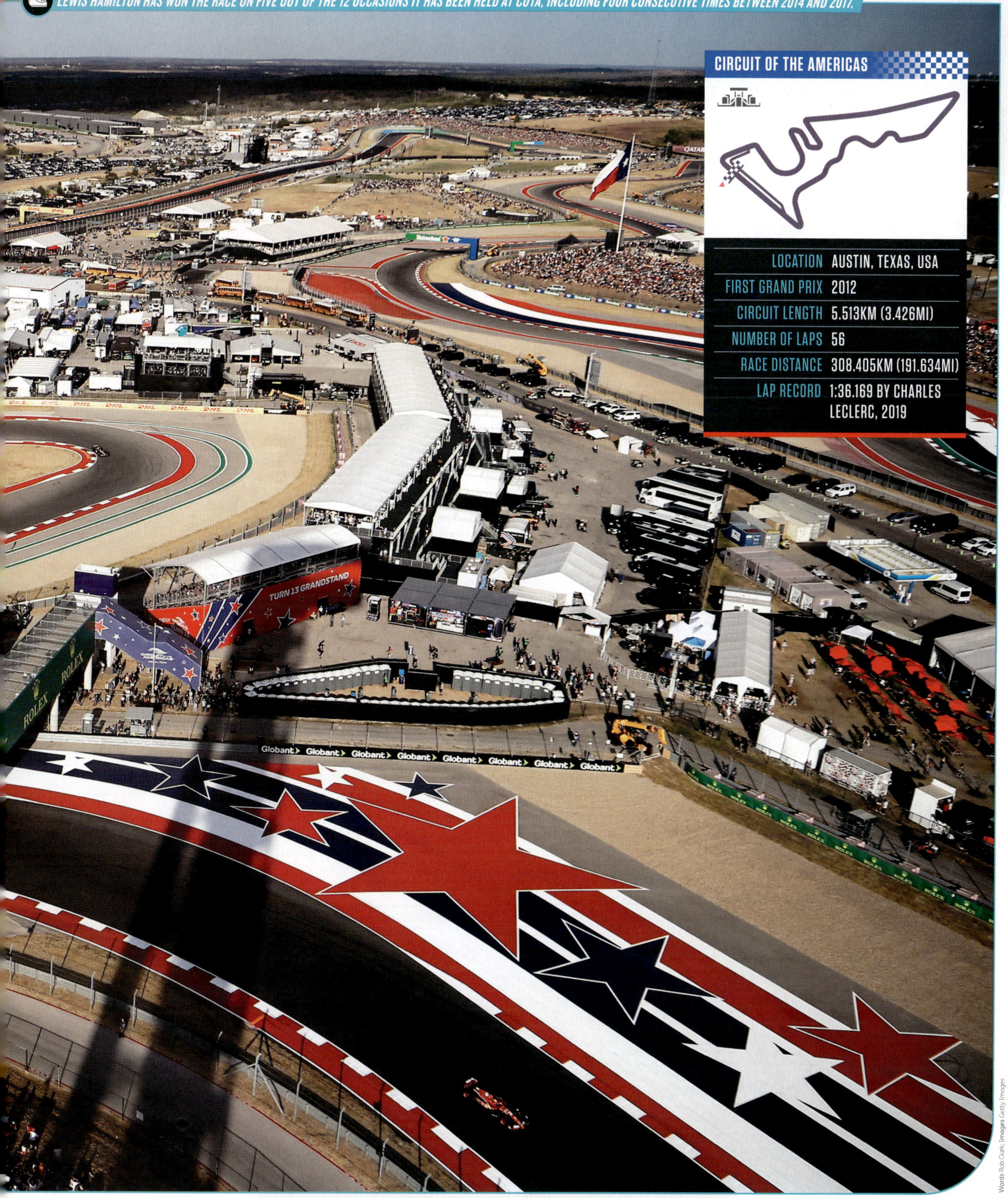

CIRCUIT OF THE AMERICAS

LOCATION	AUSTIN, TEXAS, USA
FIRST GRAND PRIX	2012
CIRCUIT LENGTH	5.513KM (3.426MI)
NUMBER OF LAPS	56
RACE DISTANCE	308.405KM (191.634MI)
LAP RECORD	1:36.169 BY CHARLES LECLERC, 2019

Words Rob Clark, Images Getty Images

MEXICO

WILL 2025 BE THE SWANSONG FOR THE MEXICO GRAND PRIX?

The Mexico Grand Prix takes place on a circuit built in 1959 in Mexico City's Magdalena Mixiuhca sports park utilising existing internal roads. The circuit isn't much different today, although the spectacular but scary Peralta corner is now bisected as the circuit weaves its way through a former baseball stadium – which affords the perfect location for viewing. F1 first came to the circuit in 1962 for a non-championship 'trial' race. This proved sufficiently successful that it was added to the official roster the following year when the Grand Prix was won by Jim Clark. There was no Mexico Grand Prix between 1993 and 2014, and, at present, the 2025 edition is set to be the last one.

THE CIRCUIT'S MOST NOTABLE FEATURE IS ITS ALTITUDE – IT SITS OVER 2KM (1.2MI) ABOVE SEA LEVEL, HIGH ENOUGH TO CAUSE SOME BREATHLESSNESS.

MEXICO

SINCE THE CIRCUIT RETURNED TO THE F1 CALENDAR IN 2015, VERSTAPPEN HAS WON FIVE OF THE NINE RACES HELD THERE.

AUTÓDROMO HERMANOS RODRÍGUEZ

LOCATION	MEXICO CITY, MEXICO
FIRST GRAND PRIX	1963
CIRCUIT LENGTH	4.304KM (2.674MI)
NUMBER OF LAPS	71
RACE DISTANCE	305.354KM (189.738MI)
LAP RECORD	1:17.774 BY VALTERRI BOTTAS, 2021

BRAZIL

BRAZIL'S INTERLAGOS CIRCUIT IS ONE OF THE BEST ON THE F1 CALENDAR

The circuit's official name is the Autódromo José Carlos Pace, but owing to its stunning location, set between two lakes purpose-built to supply the city of São Paulo with water and electricity, it has always been known as Interlagos. Built on naturally hilly terrain, the circuit has a bowl-like appearance with numerous inclines. Extensively remodelled in 1990 to address the bumpy surface, it is now fast but with numerous opportunities to overtake dotted all around the circuit. Both Hamilton and Button have sung the praises of the start-finish straight as a great place to overtake as you approach the first corner.

AS F1'S MOST FAMOUS ANTI-CLOCKWISE CIRCUIT, THE CENTRIFUGAL FORCES AT INTERLAGOS EXERT THE OPPOSITE IMPACT ON DRIVERS FROM WHAT THEY ARE USED TO.

BRAZIL

AS WITH ALL SPORTING OCCASIONS IN BRAZIL, THE GRAND PRIX COMES WITH A CARNIVAL ATMOSPHERE AND LOCAL FANS MAKE IT AN UNMISSABLE EXPERIENCE.

AUTÓDROMO JOSÉ CARLOS PACE

LOCATION	SÃO PAULO, BRAZIL
FIRST GRAND PRIX	1973
CIRCUIT LENGTH	4.309KM (2.677MI)
NUMBER OF LAPS	71
RACE DISTANCE	305.879KM (190.064MI)
LAP RECORD	1:10.540 BY VALTTERI BOTTAS, 2018

FANS & FUTURE

108 2025 SEASON PREVIEW
Looking ahead to another thrilling championship this year

122 THE F1 FANDOM
How the sport has become more popular than ever

126 THE FUTURE OF F1
What advancements and changes could F1 see in the years to come?

CIRCUITS IN FOCUS

116   LAS VEGAS
118   QATAR
120   ABU DHABI

F1 2025 SEASON PREVIEW

The stage is set: F1 celebrates its 75th anniversary with what could become a season for the ages

Words Rob Clark

The 2025 F1 season is almost upon us. As the teams and their drivers gear up for it, here's a quick guide to everything you need to know about the year ahead: the lineups, the changes and the newcomers, the new rules and regulations, and what we are looking forward to the most.

This year's calendar will feature 24 races, as it did last year, and indeed will visit all the same countries – but there have been one or two changes in the running order. The Australian Grand Prix is back to being the first race of the season, which it hasn't been since 2019. It was the third round in each of the past three seasons, after the Bahrain and Saudi Arabian Grand Prix, but this year they have been pushed to April so that those races don't take place during Ramadan.

▶

When discussing his move, Hamilton said he was fulfilling a childhood dream of "driving in Ferrari red".

F1 2025 SEASON PREVIEW

Movers and shakers

With the driver lineup now complete for 2025, some big names have switched between teams, and there are several new arrivals to look forward to. The most notable change of team is, of course, seven-time world champion Lewis Hamilton's move to Ferrari, where he will partner Charles Leclerc. The Scuderia were only 14 points off winning the Constructors' Championship last year, and will clearly be targeting that title, but can the move also reignite Hamilton's personal passion and motivation? And will his presence bring the very best out of Leclerc, or will the Monegasque be so overshadowed that his form suffers?

Liam Lawson replaces Sergio Pérez as defending champion Max Verstappen's partner, a role which has not always been an undiluted success for drivers. It seems likely that Verstappen will get preferential treatment, but Lawson could play a decisive role in the destination of the Constructors' Championship if he can regularly get into the points, and sometimes onto the podium.

> "FOR 2025, SOME BIG NAMES HAVE SWITCHED TEAMS AND THERE ARE SEVERAL NEW ARRIVALS TO LOOK FORWARD TO"

Esteban Ocon moves from Alpine to Haas, and Nico Hülkenberg joins Kick Sauber. It will be particularly interesting to see what Ocon can do as he takes over from the undeniably quick but inconsistent Kevin Magnussen (who is returning to sportscars).

As for the newcomers, Oliver Bearman will hope to build on his three 'super-sub' appearances last season with a full-time position at Haas. His former F2 teammate Kimi Antonelli steps into Hamilton's vacated seat at Mercedes, and Australian Jack Doohan replaces Ocon at Alpine. The 2024 F2 winner Gabriel Bortoleto is at Kick Sauber, and runner-up Isack Hadjar is at RB.

Pre-season testing will take place in late February at Sakhir, Bahrain.

Will 2025 see Norris become an even bigger threat to Verstappen in the Drivers' Championship?

F1 2025 SEASON PREVIEW

Time will tell if existing driver rivalries will deepen in 2025. Perhaps new ones will emerge.

Rules and regulations

Next year is when the major changes are expected – for example, this will be the 12th and last season for the V6 hybrid turbo power unit formula – and chassis regulations for 2025 will remain largely as they were last year.

Elsewhere, the minimum driver weight allowance goes up from 80 to 82kg (176 to 180lb), with a consequent increase of the overall minimum weight limit of the car (without fuel) from 798 to 800kg (1,759 to 1,763lb). The reason behind this small change was made in the interests of driver health and wellbeing. A driver cooling kit is also introduced, for use in extreme conditions (defined as over 30.5°C/86.9°F), and this will fall outside the regulations pertaining to the weight of the car – the minimum weight will increase by 5kg (11lb) when the cooling kit is present.

There will no longer be a bonus point awarded for the fastest lap. After five years, it has been decided that the fastest lap point hasn't quite delivered on its promise – to increase the entertainment value of late laps. It mainly benefited drivers who had a large gap to the car behind, and could therefore risk a late pitstop for new tyres with the sole intention of posting a fastest lap.

F1 2025 SEASON PREVIEW

Could the combination of Leclerc and Hamilton create a dream team, or lead to tensions?

> "FOR THE FIRST TIME IN ITS HISTORY, F1 WILL LAUNCH ITS NEW SEASON WITH A SPECIAL EVENT AT LONDON'S O2 ARENA"

In January 2025, Hamilton headed to Ferrari's Maranello HQ for his first test sessions.

There will be a clampdown on jump-starts and on preventing teams from sitting out rain-affected practice sessions to save tyres. Rules have also been tightened to prevent slow running during qualifying. This year, a driver's pace relative to lap time will be measured at every marshalling point.

Live launch

For the first time in the sport's history, F1 will launch its new season with a special event at London's O2 Arena where all ten teams, their principals, plus all 20 drivers, will officially unveil their 2025 liveries. In previous years, each team has decided when and where to release details of their own new-season livery, so for them to do it all together at the same time marks a significant departure.

The interactive, sold-out show will take place on the evening of 18 February and it will be streamed live in celebration of Formula 1's 75th anniversary. Expect more such events in coming seasons if this one proves to be a success.

Pre-season testing will follow from 26-28 February on the Bahrain International Circuit, and then there will be further opportunities for the teams to adjust their cars before the opening race in Melbourne on 16 March.

What's in store?

Making predictions ahead of any F1 season is always perilous, and particularly so in 2025 when there are team changes and new drivers aplenty. Verstappen will start as the man to beat, but by the end of last year, the Red Bull was no longer the fastest car on the starting grid. Both McLaren and Ferrari finished ahead of Red Bull in the Constructors' Championship and it looks likely that new teammate Liam Lawson will have to contribute if Red Bull are to stand a chance of regaining their crown.

Expect Norris to be an even bigger threat than he was in 2024, and he loomed pretty large in Verstappen's rear-view mirror then. How will the reigning champion react to not being in the fastest vehicle race in, race out…? George Russell has already shown that he is no respecter of reputations. "People have been bullied by Max for years now. He's been enabled because nobody's stood up to him," he said after the two drivers' war of words following Qatar qualifying.

> "NORRIS LOOMED PRETTY LARGE IN VERSTAPPEN'S REAR-VIEW MIRROR IN 2024. HOW WILL THE REIGNING CHAMPION REACT TO NOT BEING IN THE FASTEST VEHICLE…?"

Russell is teamed with 18-year-old Kimi Antonelli this year. Another teenager, Oliver Bearman, who impressed on an ad hoc basis last year (one race with Ferrari and two with Haas), has signed a multi-year deal with Haas. Bearman is raw, but he certainly has potential and is one to keep an eye on.

However, the biggest buzz has to be around Hamilton's move to Ferrari. The sport's most famous marque must feel it's way beyond time for them to win another Constructors' Championship – they have a record 16 of them, but none since 2008. The pairing of Hamilton and Leclerc must be odds-on favourites to put that right, as both men are more than capable of winning races and accumulating regular points if the car is competitive. The stage is set for a very interesting season indeed, and we can't wait to see it.

F2 rivals Bortoleto and Hadjar have also graduated to F1, joining Kick Sauber and Racing Bulls respectively.

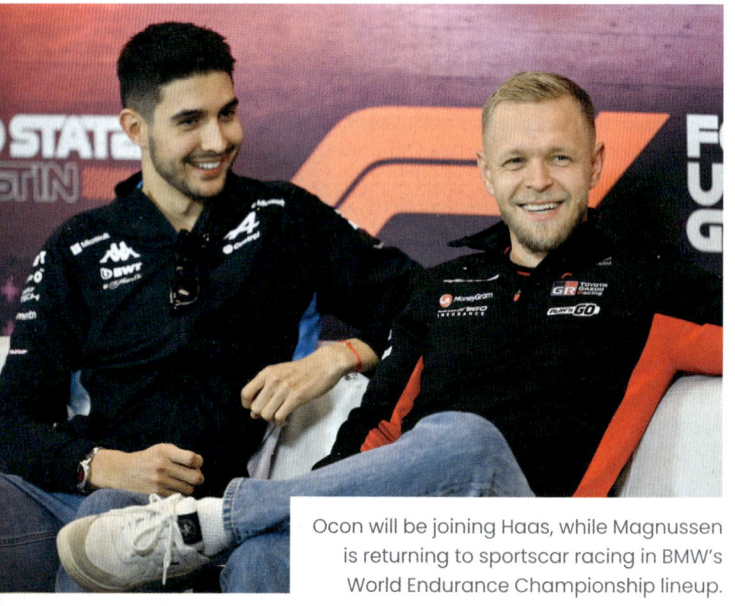

Ocon will be joining Haas, while Magnussen is returning to sportscar racing in BMW's World Endurance Championship lineup.

The Barcelona-Catalunya circuit will host the Spanish Grand Prix once more, before the event moves to a new circuit in Madrid from 2026.

F1 2025 SEASON PREVIEW

THE 2025 F1 SCHEDULE

DATE	EVENT	VENUE
26-28 FEBRUARY	PRE-SEASON TESTING	SAKHIR
14-16 MARCH	AUSTRALIAN GRAND PRIX	MELBOURNE
21-23 MARCH	CHINESE GRAND PRIX	SHANGHAI
4-6 APRIL	JAPANESE GRAND PRIX	SUZUKA
11-13 APRIL	BAHRAIN GRAND PRIX	SAKHIR
18-20 APRIL	SAUDI ARABIAN GRAND PRIX	JEDDAH
2-4 MAY	MIAMI GRAND PRIX	MIAMI, FL
16-18 MAY	EMILIA-ROMAGNA GRAND PRIX	IMOLA
23-25 MAY	MONACO GRAND PRIX	MONACO
30 MAY-1 JUNE	SPANISH GRAND PRIX	BARCELONA
13-15 JUNE	CANADIAN GRAND PRIX	MONTREAL
27-29 JUNE	AUSTRIAN GRAND PRIX	SPIELBERG
4-6 JULY	BRITISH GRAND PRIX	SILVERSTONE
25-27 JULY	BELGIAN GRAND PRIX	SPA-FRANCORCHAMPS
1-3 AUGUST	HUNGARIAN GRAND PRIX	BUDAPEST
29-31 AUGUST	DUTCH GRAND PRIX	ZANDVOORT
5-7 SEPTEMBER	ITALIAN GRAND PRIX	MONZA
19-21 SEPTEMBER	AZERBAIJAN GRAND PRIX	BAKU
3-5 OCTOBER	SINGAPORE GRAND PRIX	SINGAPORE
17-19 OCTOBER	UNITED STATES GRAND PRIX	AUSTIN, TX
24-26 OCTOBER	MEXICO CITY GRAND PRIX	MEXICO CITY
7-9 NOVEMBER	SÃO PAULO GRAND PRIX	SÃO PAULO
20-22 NOVEMBER	LAS VEGAS GRAND PRIX	LAS VEGAS, NV
28-30 NOVEMBER	QATAR GRAND PRIX	LUSAIL
5-7 DECEMBER	ABU DHABI GRAND PRIX	YAS MARINA

Former Formula 2 drivers Kimi Antonelli (left) and Oliver Bearman (right) have both graduated to full-time Formula 1 positions in 2025.

"I am super excited to work alongside Max and learn from a world champion," said Lawson.

🇺🇸 LAS VEGAS

ALL THE THRILLS OF VEGAS ADD A DIFFERENT DIMENSION TO THIS RACE

Located bang in the heart of Vegas, the Grand Prix weaves its way past numerous iconic casinos, including Caesars Palace, the Bellagio and the Venetian. The setting gives the whole event a glamour and a glitz that's hard to match, and while American fans have taken some time to warm to F1, there now appears to be a genuine appreciation for this type of racing. What American fans do require is excitement and entertainment, and the fast circuit with numerous overtaking chances provides exactly that. As a bonus, in 2024 it was the race which confirmed Verstappen (although he only finished in fifth place) as the world champion.

PRIOR TO 2023, LAS VEGAS HAD STAGED F1 RACES TWICE BEFORE, IN 1981 AND 1982, BOTH TIMES CALLED THE CAESARS PALACE GRAND PRIX.

THE RACE IS HELD ON A SATURDAY – AS A NIGHT RACE WITH A START TIME OF 10PM – BECAUSE A SUNDAY TIMESLOT WOULD BE AIRING IN THE EARLY HOURS OF MONDAY MORNING IN EUROPE.

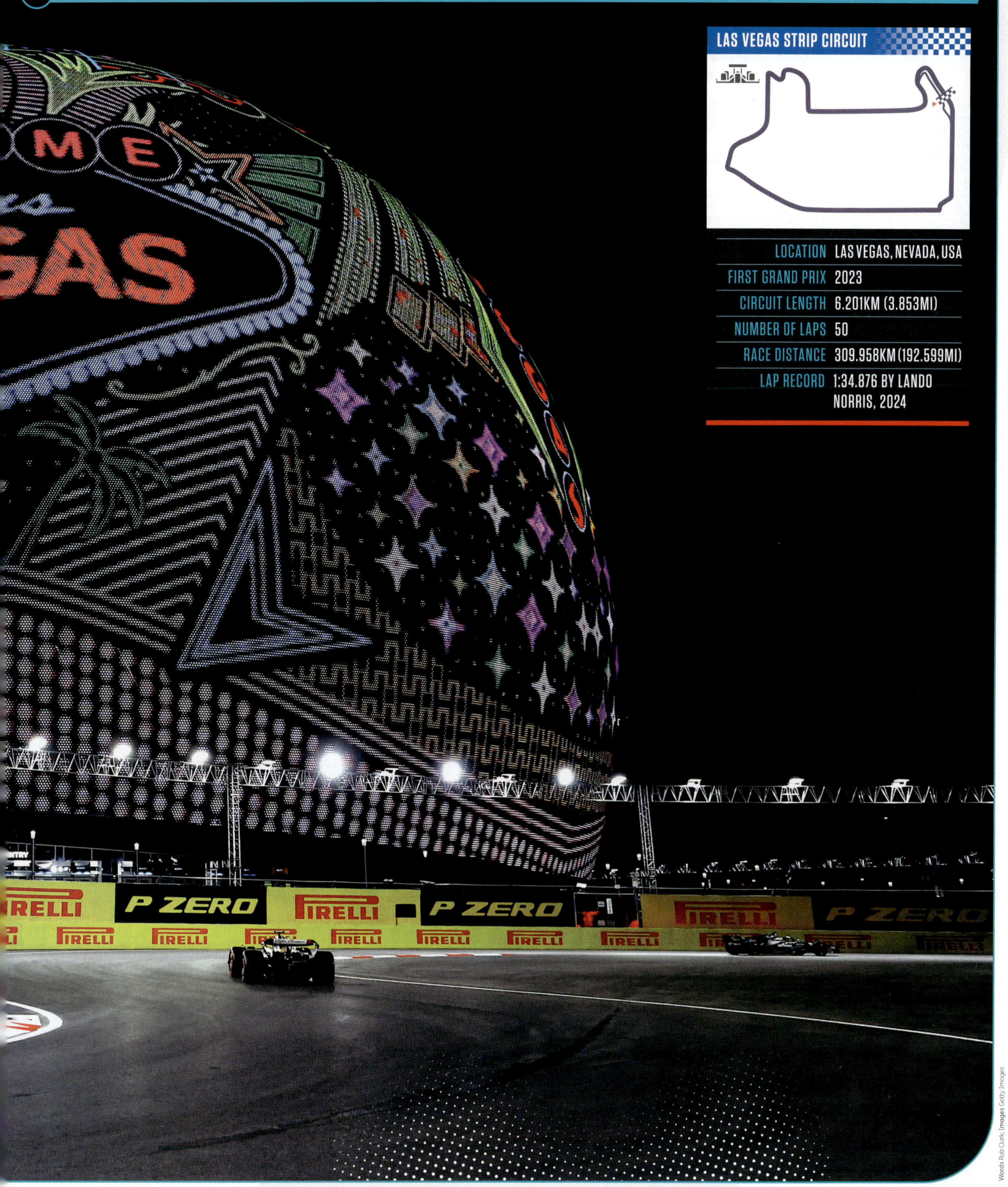

LAS VEGAS STRIP CIRCUIT

LOCATION	LAS VEGAS, NEVADA, USA
FIRST GRAND PRIX	2023
CIRCUIT LENGTH	6.201KM (3.853MI)
NUMBER OF LAPS	50
RACE DISTANCE	309.958KM (192.599MI)
LAP RECORD	1:34.876 BY LANDO NORRIS, 2024

Words Rob Clark; Images Getty Images

QATAR

ANOTHER NIGHT RACE, THE QATAR GRAND PRIX HAS FIRMLY ESTABLISHED ITSELF ON THE F1 ROSTER

The first F1 World Championship race on Qatar's Lusail International Circuit was in 2021, though MotoGP had been using it since 2004. Designed primarily for bikes, the circuit features a fast and flowing track with a succession of medium- and high-speed corners, plus a long, long (over 1km/0.62mi) opening straight into Turn 1 which affords lots of overtaking opportunities. It was the fourth race (after Singapore, Bahrain and Sakhir) to take place wholly at night, which lends a dramatic feel to events. There has been some talk of a new purpose-built circuit replacing Lusail, but those plans appear to have been shelved. The Qatar Grand Prix has a contract for ten years, up until 2033.

THE QATAR GRAND PRIX WAS NOT HELD IN 2022 BECAUSE OF THE FIFA WORLD CUP TAKING PLACE IN THE COUNTRY AT THE SAME TIME.

QATAR

PRIOR TO THE 2025 SEASON, VERSTAPPEN HAS BEEN IN THE TOP TWO IN EVERY QATAR GP – SECOND TO HAMILTON IN 2021 BEFORE WINNING IN BOTH 2023 AND 2024.

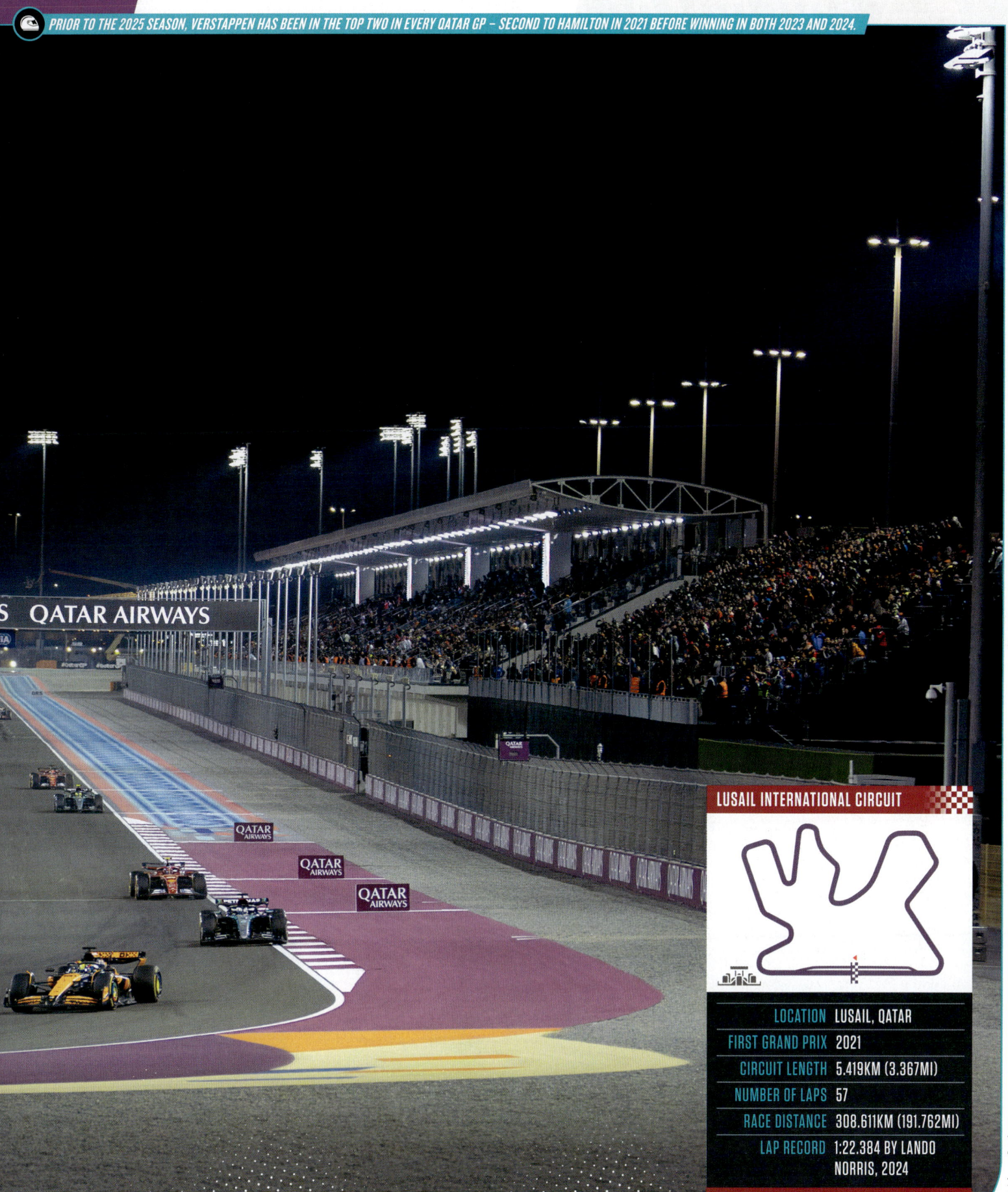

LUSAIL INTERNATIONAL CIRCUIT

LOCATION	LUSAIL, QATAR
FIRST GRAND PRIX	2021
CIRCUIT LENGTH	5.419KM (3.367MI)
NUMBER OF LAPS	57
RACE DISTANCE	308.611KM (191.762MI)
LAP RECORD	1:22.384 BY LANDO NORRIS, 2024

ABU DHABI

ABU DHABI PROVIDES A DRAMATIC SETTING FOR THE FINAL RACE OF THE 2025 CALENDAR

Debuting in 2009, the spectacular Yas Marina Circuit was purpose-built to form the central aspect of a major tourist attraction which includes hotels, a water park, a golf course, a man-made beach, a concert arena, and, above all, a Ferrari-themed park. The track itself is an interesting one, featuring several standout sections such as the long straight between Turns 5 and 6 where the slow corners at the start and finish of the straights make conditions perfect for overtaking, and the tricky, hard-braking Turns 10, 11 and 12. Some modifications in 2021 included widening certain turns to allow more speed through them.

HAMILTON HAS WON THE MOST ABU DHABI GRAND PRIX (5) BUT WAS DENIED A SIXTH IN 2021 WHEN RACE DIRECTOR MICHAEL MASI GOT THE POST-SAFETY CAR PROCEDURE WRONG.

THE RACE IS A DAY/NIGHT ONE – FLOODLIGHTS ARE ON FROM THE START TO ALLOW A SEAMLESS TRANSITION FROM DAYLIGHT TO DARKNESS, ADDING TO THE DRAMATIC FEEL.

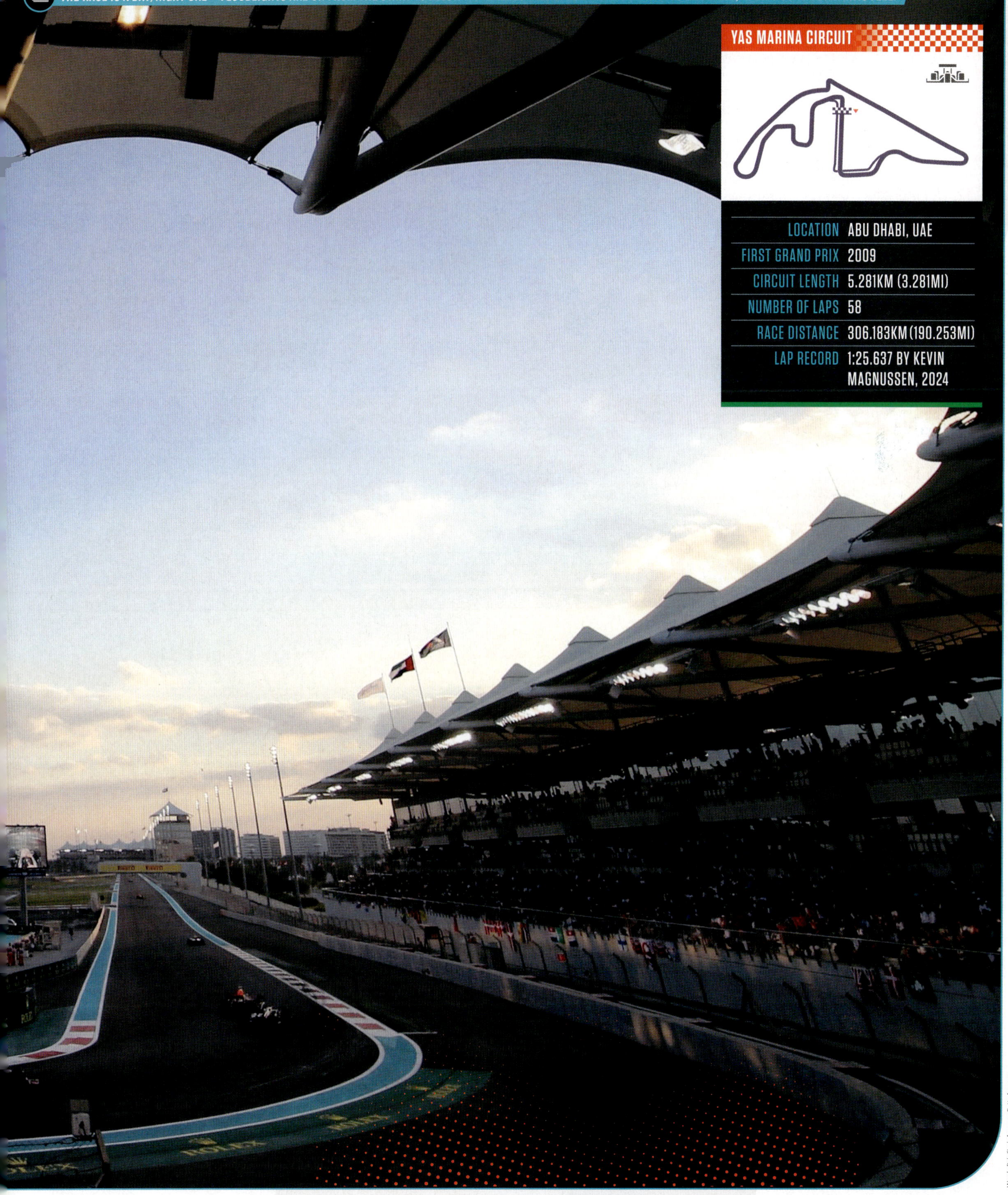

YAS MARINA CIRCUIT

LOCATION	ABU DHABI, UAE
FIRST GRAND PRIX	2009
CIRCUIT LENGTH	5.281KM (3.281MI)
NUMBER OF LAPS	58
RACE DISTANCE	306.183KM (190.253MI)
LAP RECORD	1:25.637 BY KEVIN MAGNUSSEN, 2024

Words Rob Clark. Images Getty Images

THE RISING TIDE OF F1

It's boom-time for the sport, with popularity higher than ever

Words David Smith

F1 draws in huge crowds of fans at every race weekend, come rain or shine.

THE RISING TIDE OF F1

Formula 1 has always been a glamorous sport, attracting a jet-set following, but it has recently witnessed a massive growth in popularity. The often-exotic race venues and the movie-star status of the top drivers are big attractions, as always, but several other factors are behind this current surge in interest.

In the past, although there was still an undeniable thrill in such high-stakes racing, many were put off by the staggering toll taken on the drivers – 14 of them lost their lives during the 1960s. Changes began to be made from the late Sixties onwards, leading to significantly improved safety records.

Thanks partly to this, fan numbers began to grow and it was in the 1980s that they really took off, when TV coverage expanded dramatically, bringing the races into living rooms around the world. The era of iconic drivers such as Ayrton Senna, Nigel ▶

THE RISING TIDE OF F1

Audiences in the trackside stands get to witness the race action up close.

Famous faces are a familiar sight at race weekends, with celebrity fans often spotted on the grid or touring the paddock.

The global F1 audience increased by 50 million between 2021 and 2024, with significant growth among young people and women.

THE RISING TIDE OF F1

Successful drivers often lead to a boost in the sport's popularity in their home nation.

> "THERE ARE MANY DUTCH F1 FANS WHO SAY THEIR COUNTRY HAD BASICALLY FORGOTTEN THE SPORT EXISTED UNTIL MAX VERSTAPPEN STARTED TO WIN"

Mansell and Alain Prost also boosted the profile of a sport that has always been seen more as a head-to-head encounter between drivers than a contest between the machines.

Such personalities are critical, as the most important factor in F1's success has always been its competitiveness. Exciting races and championships have always been the main motivator for fan engagement, and surprisingly competitive races (seven different drivers won at least one Grand Prix) added an extra layer of excitement to the 2024 season.

This continued a trend seen since Liberty Media took control of the sport in 2017. Long the preserve of petrol heads, the new owners wanted to transform F1's fan base, expanding it by making the sport more accessible and more understandable.

Of huge importance in this process was the launch of the Netflix show *Drive to Survive*, which has attracted millions of viewers since it debuted in 2019. We had often been given teasing glimpses 'under the hood' of F1, but through this series we could watch teams struggle with their equipment and each other in a documentary that was often shocking in its openness. Personal rivalries between team principals, clashes between drivers and the never-ending quest to drag an extra split-second of performance out of a thoroughbred racing machine made for compelling viewing and created a new generation of informed and passionate fans.

Local heroes

From country to country, the popularity of the sport tends to ebb and flow with the success of native drivers – there are many Dutch F1 fans who say their country had basically forgotten the sport existed until Max Verstappen started to win races and then championships.

The sport has also recently been helped by the ability to tap into the lucrative US market. Americans love their cars, and while NASCAR and IndyCar retain their places at the top of the tree, F1 is gaining in popularity. The addition of Miami and Las Vegas Grands Prix, in 2022 and 2023 respectively, not only increased exposure in the States, they also opened up new sponsorship and advertising revenues.

As might be expected, the Americans know how to exploit a commercial opportunity, and with many F1 fans coming from wealthy demographics, there is the potential to tap into that wealth. At the 2023 Las Vegas Grand Prix, for instance, Paddock Club tickets were available at $15,000 each, offering great viewing positions, as well as unlimited food and drink over a five-day experience.

If that isn't exclusive (or expensive) enough, fans can also go to F1 Experiences to sign up for the ultimate package. If you have around $25,000-$35,000 to spare, you can indulge yourself in the F1 Garage package, which includes access to the F1 paddock, a guided tour of the track, pitlane walks as the teams prepare for practice, qualifying and races, and of course all the Michelin-star cuisine and champagne you could wish for. It's hard to think how you could get closer to F1 without starting your own team.

There are signs that the boost in viewer numbers has plateaued following the initial, stunning successes since Liberty Media took over the sport. If that proves to be the case, it is a safe bet that new initiatives will be tried to get the numbers trending upwards again. F1 is not a sport that stands still in any area.

THE FUTURE OF F1

In a restless sport, change is always in the air.

What could we see in the years ahead?

Words David Smith

SUSTAINABLE FUELS

The sport dipped its toe in this area in 2022, asking for 10% of fuels to be ethanol, but fully sustainable fuels will be mandatory for the 2026 season. The sport claims that the fuel it is developing will also be compatible with most road cars in the world.

SLIMMING DOWN

F1 cars are big and heavy, but they are about to be put on a diet, with the aim being to trim 40-50kg (88-110lb). A smaller wheelbase will result in lighter, sleeker-looking cars, and the reduction in weight will boost responsiveness and help reduce tyre wear.

THE FUTURE OF F1

NET-ZERO CARBON

The sustainable fuel move is just part of F1's commitment to create net-zero carbon emissions by 2030. The initiative will include more careful planning of the F1 calendar (to lessen the impact of travel and freight shipping), a reduction in the use of single-use plastics and the introduction of renewable energy in offices.

AN INCLUSIVE SPORT

In years to come, we may start to see the impact of F1's diversity and inclusion charter. The sport has launched initiatives to help address issues of underrepresentation on the track, in the paddock, and behind the scenes. This includes a variety of projects, from STEM outreach and engineering scholarships to increased support in grassroots karting.

NEW CIRCUITS

The F1 calendar is crammed to bursting, but new circuits have a shot of inclusion when existing tracks drop out, or if rotations are introduced. From 2026, the Spanish Grand Prix will be hosted at a new circuit in Madrid, and there is a real appetite to introduce a street race in Bangkok, possibly as soon as 2027. The sport would also love to return to Africa, since the last South African Grand Prix was held in 1993.

NEW TEAMS

There is no shortage of people wanting to launch new teams, and it is hoped that an 11th constructor will soon take its place on the starting grid. General Motors, in the form of Cadillac, is expected to be approved for racing in 2026. Plans have also been floated for more new teams, which could possibly join on a trial basis and compete in a limited number of races for their first seasons, pending full admittance.

GOING ELECTRIC

This may be a longer shot, but F1 already utilises hybrid technology and is looking into the use of fully electric engines. The use of sustainable fuels is expected to take precedence for now, but the future may well be electric. This would inevitably lead to questions regarding a potential takeover or merger with the existing Formula E championship.

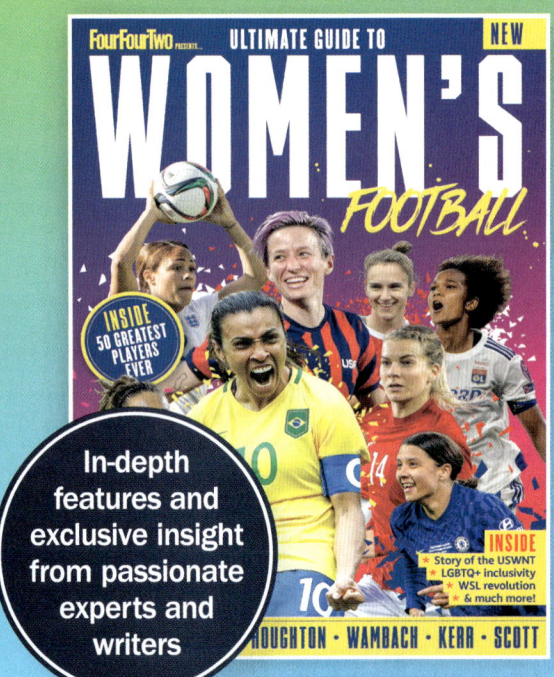
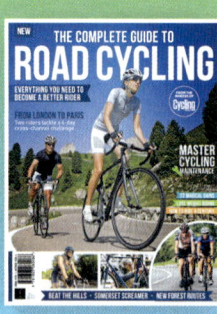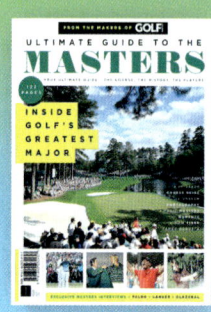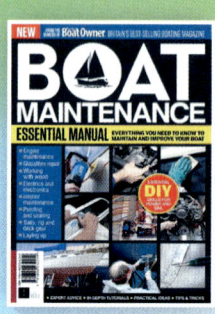

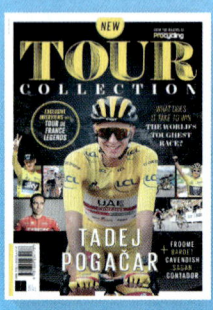
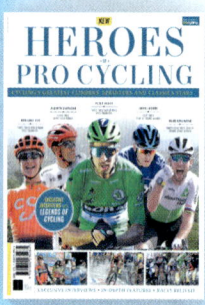

In-depth features and exclusive insight from passionate experts and writers

Explore the darker side of sport, where the will to win can hide a multitude of sins

Discover everything there is to know about your favourite teams and players

 Get great savings when you buy direct from us

 1000s of great titles, many not available anywhere else

 World-wide delivery and super-safe ordering

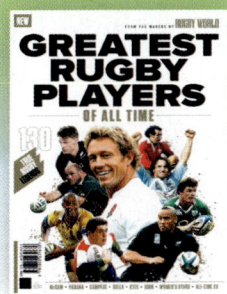
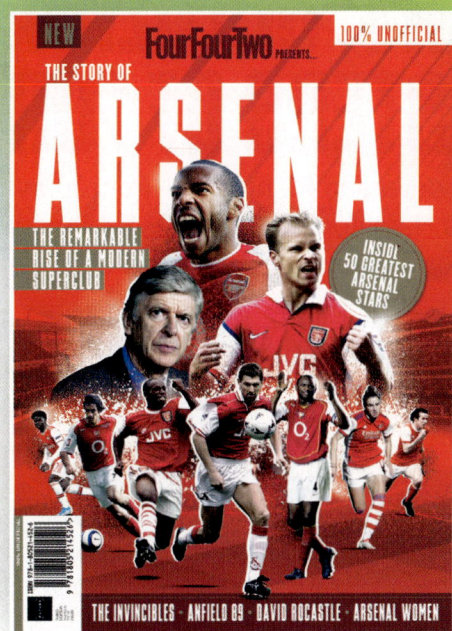

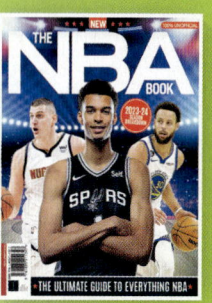

SPORT BOOKAZINES AT THEIR BEST

Whether you're a football fan, want to improve your golf, love all things NBA or follow the NFL, we've got you covered…

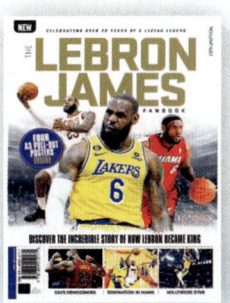
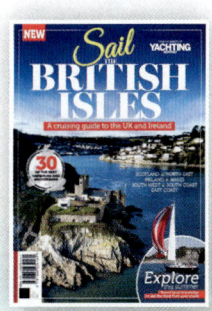

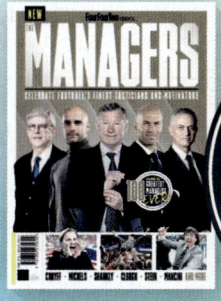

Relive great players, iconic moments and revolutionary managers

Follow us on Instagram @futurebookazines

Future

www.magazinesdirect.com/sport

Magazines, back issues & bookazines.